Following Chopin

Liliana Olchowik-Adamowska
Kazimierz Kunicki
Tomasz Ławecki

Photographs
Waldemar Panów
Zbigniew Panów

Following Chopin
The Guide

BOSz

Table of contents

Chopin

Fryderyk Chopin was twenty years old when he left Poland on the eve of the November Uprising in 1830, never to return to his homeland again. After his death, only his heart was brought back to Warsaw. During his life in Poland he had had just two permanent addresses: one was his birthplace in Żelazowa Wola, where he had spent his infancy and which he had visited several times afterwards to see the family of Count Skarbek, and the other is Warsaw.

There are many places and historic buildings in the Polish capital inextricably tied to and immediately identified with the figure of Chopin, such the Royal Baths Park, with its statue of the composer, the Holy Cross church where his heart rests, the Chopin family drawing-room at the Czapski-Krasiński Palace, the Gniński-Ogiński Palace, which houses the Chopin Museum, or the National Philharmonic Hall – the scene of the world-famous International Fryderyk Chopin Piano Competition, held there every five years. However, the traces of the composer's presence, preserved in many different ways, can also be found in other, less obvious locations. The bicentennial of his birth has given rise to new initiatives related to his legacy, and this guide aspires to bring to you not only the existing and the most recently established, but also the already planned and soon to be completed, monuments of his great heritage.

During the seven years of his teenage youth Chopin managed to traverse and get to know many different regions of Poland – from Gdańsk to Cracow, to Poznań and Wrocław. It seems a surprisingly extensive itinerary for the routine holiday trips of a young student, especially if one realizes that his were the times when the only available means of travel was by horse-drawn vehicle: carriage, buggy, or coach. Almost all of his journeys were of a social nature, and although Chopin's companions would sometimes be his parents, as during a holiday in Duszniki, or a family friend, as in the case of the "naturalist" with whom he had visited Berlin, he most often traveled in the company of his young friends and their relatives, staying at their family residences. Everywhere he went he was greeted with warmth and open arms. Consistently fêted for his virtuosic piano performances, he always readily obliged when asked to enliven the ambiance of his hosts' salons with his playing.

In his travels he appears to have predominantly covered the central and western parts of the country. Apart from a trip to an estate in the province of Lublin, he had never visited any other part of eastern Poland, much less the far Eastern Borderlands, with their cities of Vilnius and Lviv. It would appear that the directions of his travels were simply determined by where his parents', and later, his own friends had happened to live.

As for "Chopin the traveller," he was reportedly a keen and receptive one, of which the best evidence is his voluminous (despite not being complete), evocative espistolograhy, and, most of all, his music in which these experiences, filtered through his creative genius, seem to incessantly echo.

This compact guide offers a brief itinerary of Chopin's travels around Poland. In order to make it truly tourist-friendly, instead of in a chronological order we have arranged them according to the regions he visited. For better orientation, each region is illustrated with a detailed map (including Warsaw, Masovia, Dobrzyń and Chełmo Regions, Silesia, Greater Poland and Lesser Poland), with clearly marked trails of Chopin's voyages to Duszniki, Gdańsk, to Berlin via Greater Poland, to Vienna via Lesser Poland, and to Poturzyn in the province of Lublin.

Chopin's Poland – by stagecoach with the composer

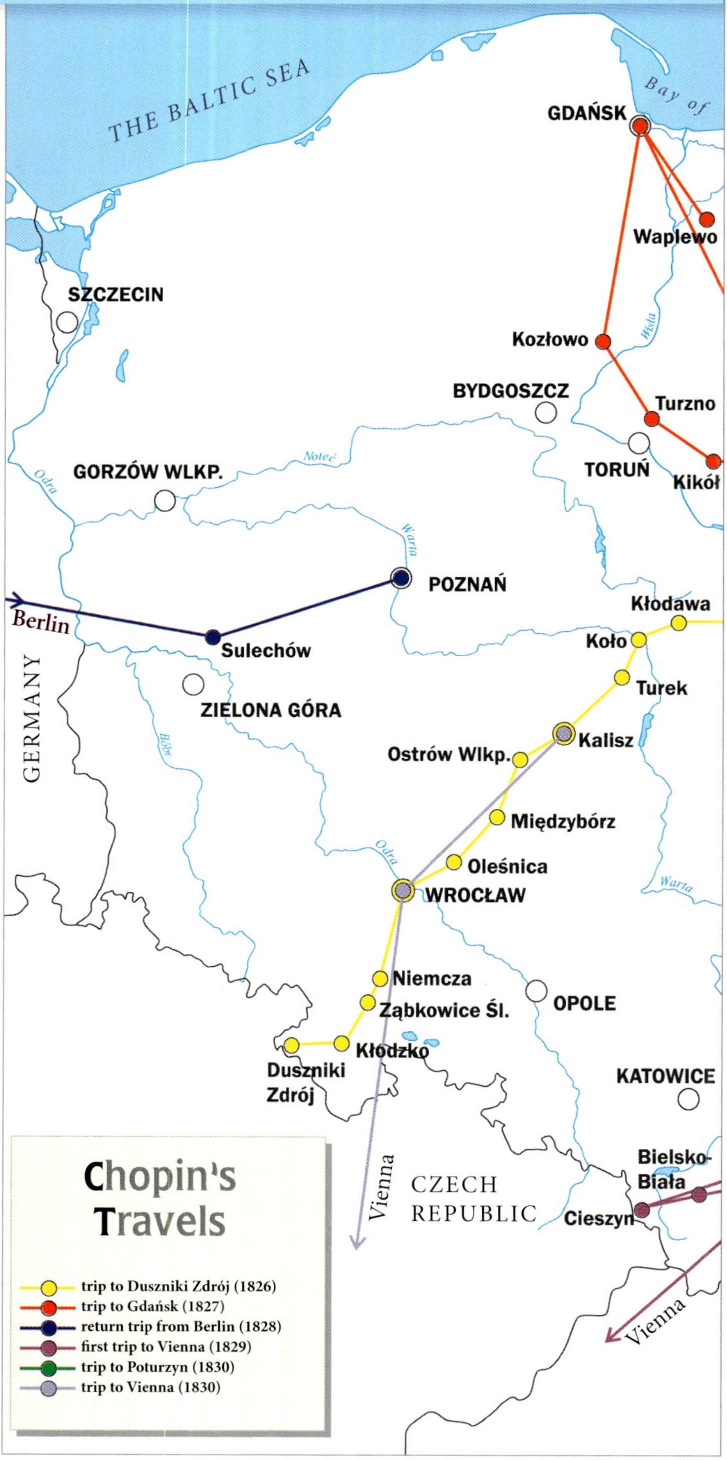

RUSSIA
LITHUANIA
Gdańsk
OLSZTYN
BIAŁYSTOK
Narew
Rościszewo
Kowalewo
Płock
Wisła
Bug
BELARUS
Kutno
Sochaczew
WARSAW
Piaseczno
Błonie
Łowicz
Czersk
ŁÓDŹ
Pilica
Kozienice
Puławy
Wieprz
Opoczno
Końskowola
LUBLIN
Końskie
Krasnystaw
KIELCE
Zamość
Poturzyn
San
Pieskowa Skała
Ojców
Wisła
CRACOW
Wieliczka
RZESZÓW
Wadowice
UKRAINE
SLOVAKIA

1823

Chopin spends part of his summer holidays in **Żelazowa Wola**, staying with the Skarbek family, whom he had visited on several other occasions; he also supposedly – according to unverified information – passes some of the time with the Marylski family, in their estate in **Pęcice** near Warsaw

1824

August–September. Chopin vacations in **Szafarnia**, in the province of Dobrzyń, at the home of a school friend, Dominik Dziewanowski. In his letters of the period he describes the villages and estates he had visited. The traces of his presence have been preserved in **Sokołowo** (estate of the Wybraniecki family), **Gulbiny** (the Piwnickis' mansion estate), **Ugoszcz** (the palace of the Borzewski family), **Obory** (the Carmelite monastery), **Obrowo** (the mansion estate of the Romockis), **Golub** and **Nieszawa**.

1825

August. Second holiday in the **Szafarnia** area. Chopin visits **Turzno**, staying at the Działowskis' mansion estate. He takes a trip to see **Toruń**.

1826

July 28. Chopin leaves for **Duszniki** with his mother and sisters, Ludwika and Emilia. The coach route leads through **Błonie**, **Sochaczew**, **Łowicz**, **Kutno**, **Kłodawa**, **Koło**, **Turek**, **Kalisz**, **Ostrów**, **Międzybórz**, **Oleśnica**, **Wrocław**, **Niemcza**, **Ząbkowice** and **Kłodzko**.

August 2–September 11. The stay at the Duszniki health resort. On his return trip home he stops in **Wrocław** from **13-15 September**.

1827

July–August. A several-weeks' trip to **Gdańsk**, via **Płock**. *"So today in **Płock**, tomorrow in **Rościszewo**, the day after in **Kikół**, then stay for a few days in **Turzno**, a couple in **Kozłów**, then quickly off to **Gdańsk**, turn around, and start back home"*. While in Gdańsk, he visists the Sierakowskis in **Waplewo**. *En route* to Warsaw he stops at the Zboinski family estate in **Kowalewo**.

1828

July–August. Chopin spends the summer in **Sanniki**, near Płock, at the house of a school friend, Constantine Pruszak.

September 9. Chopin sets out to Berlin, accompanying his father's friend Feliks Jarocki, a participant of the international Berlin conference of the "naturalists." On **September 29** on the return trip, he gives an improvised piano performance during a coach stopover in **Sulechów Wielkopolski** (this information has recently been deemed unreliable). **Early October** – a short stay in **Poznań**.

1829

Mid July. Chopin sets off on his first trip to Vienna. The route leads through **Opoczno**, **Końskie**, **Cracow**, **Wadowice**, **Bielsko**, **Cieszyn**.
July 23, he writes, "*The first week was passed sightseeing in Cracow and touring the area around it.*"
He is in awe of **Ojców** and **Pieskowa Skała**.
October 21. He stays in **Strzyżew**, near Poznań, visiting his godmother, Anna Wiesiołowska, *nee* Skarbek. He is invited by Duke Radziwiłł for a weeks' stay at his summer residence in **Antonin**.
Early November. On the return trip he stops in **Kalisz** (at doctor Adam Heblich's) and **Żychlin** (at the Bronikowskis' palace).

1830

July 10-20. Chopin travels to **Poturzyn** in the Lublin province, where he visits the family of Tytus Woyciechowski. The route leads through **Piaseczno**, **Czersk**, **Kozienice**, **Puławy**, **Końskowola**, **Lublin**, **Krasnystaw** and **Zamość**.
August 29. Chopin is invited by general Piotr Szembek, a great lover of the violin music, "a rabid Paganinist," to perform and improvise at the military training camp in **Sochaczew**.
November 2. Four weeks before the outbreak of the November Uprising Chopin leaves Warsaw for Vienna, seen off by a crowd of friends, professors and relatives who had gathered at the border-town inn in Wola to bid him farewell. On **November 4** his friend Tytus Woyciechowski joins him in **Kalisz** and they continue the journey together.
From **November 6-9** they stay in **Wrocław**, where Chopin gives a recital at the Guildhouse and meets with local musicians.

(Based on the *Calendarium of Chopin's Life*, courtesy of the Chopin Internet Information Centre, available on the official Fryderyk Chopin Institute website)

Mazovian willows

FRYDERYK CHOPIN'S WARSAW

Chopin spent the whole first half of his life in Warsaw. Only a few buildings from his times have survived unscathed to the present: the St. Joseph's the Betrothed church of the Nuns of the Visitation, Belvedere, Kazimierz Palace, the Royal Baths Park, and the Saxon Garden – "the Botanika," as it was nicknamed by young Fryderyk. Others, like the Krasiński or Staszic palaces were reconstructed after World War II, while some less fortunate ones, including the Saxon Palace, have never been rebuilt.

Over the years numerous new sites and venues have come into being along the memorial route of Chopin's Warsaw, embossing, as the poet Cyprian Kamil Norwid had once worded it, the profile of the Master. It is impossible nowadays to imagine Warsaw without the art-nouveaux monument to the composer in the Royal Baths Park, his Museum at the Gniński-Ostrogski Palace, or the Warsaw National Philharmonic Hall, the venue of the International Fryderyk Chopin Piano Competition. He has been given his own street here, schools have chosen him as their patron, and, last but not least, the Warsaw airport in Okęcie is named Fryderyk Chopin Airport.

The Castle Square in Warsaw – in a period engraving (above) and in a contemporary photograph; in the foreground is King Sigismund's Column, on the right – the Royal Castle

The King John III Sobieski monument in the Royal Baths Park

Warsaw
Places associated with Chopin

WYSZKÓW 629
801 LEGIONOWO
719 SIEDLCE
KARCZEW 801
631 SIEDLCE
Wisła
OKRZEI
ZAMOYSKIEGO
WYBRZEŻE SZCZECIŃSKIE
DOBRA
FURMAŃSKA
BROWARNA
WYBRZEŻE KOŚCIUSZKOWSKIE
MOST ŚWIĘTOKRZYSKI
SOKOLA
BOTANIKA (KAZIMIERZ PARK)
THE VISITANDINES' CHURCH
KAZIMIERZ PALACE
RADNA
WAŁ MIEDZIESZYŃSKI
LOGOS
STASZIC PALACE
TAMKA
FRYDERYK CHOPIN MUSEUM
MOST PONIATOWSKIEGO
NOWY ŚWIAT
PARK IM. K. BEYERA
AL. JEROZOLIMSKIE
ROYAL ROUTE RESIDENCE
PARK IM. MARSZ. RYDZA-ŚMIGŁEGO
LUDOWA
OKRĄG
NEW HOTEL
BRACKA
KSIĄŻĘCA
PLAC TRZECH KRZYŻY
WILANOWSKA
SHERATON
CZERNIAKOWSKA
POWIŚLE
SOLEC
GRAND
WIEJSKA
ROZBRAT
KRUCZA
WILCZA
GÓRNOŚLĄSKA
AL. UJAZDOWSKI
KOZIŃSKA
PIĘKNA
MOKOTOWSKA
CHOPINA
PARK UJAZDOWSKI
JAZDÓW
AL. ARMII LUDOWEJ
ŁAZIENKOWSKA
KOSZYKOWA
PLAC ZBAWICIELA
AL. WYZWOLENIA
MYŚLIWIECKA
AGRYKOLA
PARK ŁAZIENKOWSKI
SZWOLEŻERÓW
MARSZAŁKOWSKA
AL. SZUCHA
AL. UJAZDOWSKIE
POLNA
FRYDERYK CHOPIN MONUMENT
ŁAZIENKI PALACE
PLAC UNII LUBELSKIEJ
BAGATELA
BELVEDERE

Shortly after Fryderyk was born (or, Frycek, as he was called in the family), Mikołaj Chopin permanently moved to Warsaw.

Jarosław Iwaszkiewicz, *Chopin*

In September of 1810 Mikołaj Chopin had been offered a teaching position at the Warsaw Lyceum, and the family, with the six-month-old baby Frycek and his elder sister Ludwika, moved into the second-floor apartment in the right wing of the Saxon Palace, which had housed the school since 1817. In this flat, facing Krakowskie Przedmieście Street, Chopin's parents ran a boarding-house for schoolboys, one of who, Jan Białobłocki, would become one of Frycek's dearest friends.

The neighbourhood, with a lush Saxon Garden just a short distance away, was ideal for a mother of two young children like Justyna Chopin. When Frycek was seven, the family moved again, this time to Kazimierz Palace. However, even as a teenager Chopin would often return to the beloved park of his early childhood. He may have also visited it in the company of the object of his first romantic raptures, Konstancja Gładkowska.

The Saxon Palace was erected at the outset of the 18th century by King August II the Strong, when several once separate residences, previously owned by the magnate families of the Lubomirskis, Sapiehas and Morsztyns, respectively, were remodelled and joined together to create a stylistically uniform single building. In 1797 the Saxon Palace became the property of the Russian oppressors. In 1839-1842 its middle section was rebuilt and a Corinthian-style colonnade was added on, below which the Polish government established a symbolic Tomb of the Unknown Soldier in 1925. The Palace itself was destroyed during World War II, and the only trace of its existence now is the memorial monument rebuilt in 1946. Ashes of anonymous soldiers have been laid to rest there, along with earth from historic battlefields – from Cedynia to World War II sites. Every Sunday a solemn changing of the guard is celebrated there to commemorate those who have given their lives for their country.

In the years 1713-1733 a park, henceforth to be known as the Saxon Garden, was created behind the Palace, following the designs of Jan K. Naumann and Mateusz D. Poppelmann, who had favoured the formal, symmetrical French style. In the days of Chopin's youth, the Garden, which in 1727 had become Warsaw's first public park, was rearranged in the manner of an English garden, emulating a natural landscape. The neoclassical Water Tower and the Empire-style fountain in the shape of a chalice date from 1854-1855, and were designed by Henryk Marconi. Nowadays adjacent to the Piłsudski Square, the Saxon Garden still boasts some of the original plant specimens which Chopin in his time must have admired, such as the gingko biloba trees imported in the 18th century from China and Japan, or the original Baroque renderings of the Muses and Virtues sculpted in sandstone by Jan Jerzy Plersch. The marble sundial near the fountain was installed in 1863. The two statues nearby represent the 19th century writer and poet Maria Konopnicka (1966, by Stanisław Kulon) and Stefan Starzyński, Warsaw's heroic wartime president (1981, by Ludwika Nitschowa).

The Saxon Garden in Autumn

The Saxon Palace and Garden

The Saxon Garden and the Tomb of the Unknown Soldier

Dearest Papa!
Though it would have been far easier for me to express my love with music, yet realising that even the most exquisite recital wouldn't contain all of my affection for you, dearest Papa, I must trust my humble heart to provide words which are as true as they are simple, to declare to you my fondest gratitude and deepest filial devotion.

Fryderyk Chopin to his father,
December 6, 1818

In March of 1817 the family moved into an apartment in the left-hand annex of the Kazimierz Palace. It was there that they celebrated Mikołaj Chopin's name day, on which occasion the eight-year-old Frycek, already showing outstanding musical talent, recited these greetings. The spacious second-floor flat, just as the previous one in the Saxon Palace, had been turned into a boarding house for boys from noble families who were getting their education in Warsaw. From the memoirs of the tenants the Chopins' home emerges as a modest, but warm and friendly place. Some of the boys, just like Fryderyk, were students at the Warsaw Lyceum, and he had made several friends in this way, including Jan Matuszyński, Dominik Dziewanowski and Tytus Woyciechowski, whom he had already met some years before.

The Kazimierz Palace at 26/32 Krakowskie Przedmieście used to be the summer residence of Queen Maria Ludwika Gonzaga, the wife of King John II Casimir. It was erected in 1634 and rebuilt in 1765 on the orders of King Stanislaus Augustus Poniatowski in the late neoclassical fashion, to house the School of Knights (1765-1795), the first state Corps of Cadets in the Polish-Lithuanian Commonwealth. For a brief period, from 1816 to 1817, the building accommodated the Royal Warsaw University, and then it was turned over to the Warsaw Lyceum.

Today the main quarters of the Kazimierz Palace are occupied by the Warsaw University authorities, and the left, "Chopin" extension houses the Institute of Oriental Sciences and the Institute of Art History. On the front wall, on the first-floor level, there is a plaque commemorating the master's stay, with an inscription: *Fryderyk Chopin lived in this house during the years 1817-1827*. Next to the plaque is a relief likeness of Chopin, reproduced from a locket designed by J.F.A. Bovy.

The Kazimierz Palace – Home and School

Entrance gate to Warsaw University, with the Rector's office in the former Kazimierz Palace

Kazimierz Palace; below, Krakowskie Przedmieście Street, view from the main University building

The Warsaw University registration book with the Chopins' entry

The Warsaw University Museum

My Botanic Garden, this old annexe behind the palace, has been beautifully spruced up by the Commission. No more carrots (…), sofas, gazebos, no lettuce, cabbage, or other foul odours etc, just flowerbeds…

Fryderyk Chopin to Jan Białobłocki,
May 15, 1826

The botanic garden, to which Fryderyk referred as "the Botanika," stretched just behind the Kazimierz Palace. In one of his letters to Jaś Białobłocki young Frycek writes that his parents have a key to the adjoining garden, which is his daily playground. He would come here also as a Lyceum student to read, and in his Conservatory years, for romantic walks with Konstancja Gładkowska.

Konstancja Gładkowska (1810-1889), an opera singer, the great love of Chopin's youth

The 19th-century Kazimierz park, situated between a cluster of the University's buildings and Oboźna, Browarna and Karowa streets, is still here. Every day throngs of students cross it on their way from the library to the university campus in Krakowskie Przedmieście. In 2007-2009 the garden was revitalised and enclosed, and regained its original character (the main entrance gate is at Browarna street, facing Lipowa Street). Next to old trees young saplings, herbs and roses have been planted, and even a stream has been added, which now cascades its way down from the foot of the Kazimierz Palace. Old-fashioned flowerbeds and smooth lawns, gravel paths and inviting benches seem to evoke the slow-paced, romantic times of Fryderyk Chopin.

Walking in the "Botanika"

Picturesque steps near Kazimierz Park

A flowerbed in Kazimierz Park

A gable room has already been done up for my convenience, with a stair leading up from the dressing-room. I am to have my old pianoforte put there, along with my old writing desk, and it is going to be my sanctuary.

Fryderyk Chopin to Tytus Woyciechowski, December 1827

In 1827 Fryderyk's youngest sister, the fourteen-year-old Emilia, died of tuberculosis and the Chopins moved again, to a rented apartment in the Czapski-Krasiński Palace at 5 Krakowskie Przedmieście. In the left wing they occupied Fryderyk was given a study of his own, the gable room he mentions in the letter to his friend. Here he could focus, undisturbed, on writing music, and studying for his classes at the High School of Music, which was run by Józef Elsner. The apartment was directly across from the main University gate and Fryderyk's friends would often drop by to see him on their way to or from classes.

The palace, erected in the years 1713-1718, was built on the site of the 17th-century wooden Radziwiłł mansion. It frequently changed tenants and owners, and in the course of time was the residence of some of the finest aristocratic families in Poland, such as the Radziwiłłs, Sieniawskis, Czartoryskis, Czapskis, Małachowskis and Krasińskis. In 1752-1765 the Czapskis renovated the building in the late Baroque style, and the gate was enhanced with two stone lions. In 1790 the next owner – Konstancja, the wife of the Marshal of the Four-Year Sejm, Stanisław Małachowski – commissioned the architect and interior decorator, Jan Chrystian Kamsetzer, to add two neoclassical extensions to the building. In 1809 the palace became the property of the Krasiński family, and at one point was home to the poet Zygmunt Krasiński, who later became one of the three greatest poets of Polish Romanticism, known as the Three Bards. It also used to house the school where another great poet, Cyprian Kamil Norwid, received education. In 1930 on the palace's left wing, on the front wall facing Krakowskie Przedmieście street, a memorial plaque was placed, bearing the following inscription: *In this house Fryderyk Chopin lived and worked before leaving Warsaw forever in 1830.*

After World War II the Kazimierz palace was reconstructed in the original neoclassical style and by the decision of the Polish government became the venue of the Academy of Fine Arts. Its baroque courtyard, surrounded by neoclassical facades of tenement houses, is set off by a copy of a statue by Verocchio, depicting Colleoni, a Venetian condotierro. In 1960, in the left wing where Fryderyk Chopin and his family used to live, the Chopins' drawing-room was recreated, based on the 1832 sketches the composer's friend, Antoni Kolberg, sent to him in Paris. Despite the lack of actual family mementoes, the 19th-century furniture accurately evokes the spirit of the times, and the two grand pianos, a Buchholz and an Erard, along with the smaller Pleyel instrument seem to bring back the days when the apartment's walls resonated with the sounds of orchestra rehearsals and witnessed musical soirees attended by friends, musicians and publicists, thrilled to be among the chosen few to listen to pre-premiere renditions of Chopin's concertos for the pianoforte, performed by the composer himself. The drawing-room walls are hung with numerous portraits of the master's family, his teachers, and views of 19th-century Warsaw.

The Drawing-Room in the Krasiński Palace

The front of the former Kazimierz Palace – currently the Academy of Fine Arts

The Chopins' appartment in Antoni Kolberg's drawing, dated 1832

The Chopin's drawing-room at the Czapski/Krasiński Palace

I have now become the Lyceum organist. (…) Well, my Good Sir, what do you say to that! I am now the first personage in the whole Lyceum, just after the Reverend! I play on the organ every week at Sunday mass at the Visitandines, and the crowd sings.

Fryderyk Chopin to Jan Białobłocki, November 1825

Attendance at the Sunday service at the church of the Nuns of the Visitation at 34 Krakowskie Przedmieście Street was compulsory for all Lyceum pupils and University students, and so for Fryderyk too. In 1825 he also started playing the organ at mass there, which, judging from his letter to Jan Białobłocki, filled him with great joy. Starting the following autumn, already a student at the High School of Music, he would give regular recitals there, mostly at religious festivals, and accompany at the students' mass on Sunday, often performing with the choir and soloists of the Conservatory, under the direction of Józef Elsner. St. Joseph the Betrothed Church is locally referred to as the Nuns of the Visitation church, or simply "the Visitandines." The church and convent were built for the nuns brought to Poland from France by queen Maria Ludwika Gonzaga. Construction started in 1654, to a design by Karol Bay, but was completed only over a hundred years later, in 1763 under the supervision of Efraim Schroeger. During World War II it managed to escape the fate of most of Warsaw's historic buildings, which were either heavily damaged or completely destroyed. It has retained the original Baroque facade, adorned with sculptures by Jan Jerzy Plersch. The rich late Baroque and rococo interior boasts a mid-18th-century boat-shaped pulpit, impressive main altar sculptures and an ebony tabernacle, bequeathed in 1654 by Queen Maria Ludwika – it is a gem of the 17th-century French craftsmanship, decorated with miniature silver plaques by Herman Pothoff. In the main altar *The Visitation*, a painting by Tadeusz Kuntze-Konicz, attracts attention, while the first altar in the main aisle is decorated with *St. Francis de Sales*, by Szymon Czechowicz.

In 1987 a monument by Andrzej Renes was raised on the square in front of the Visitandines' church to honour the memory of Primate of the Millennium, Cardinal Stefan Wyszyński. It is also at this church that the beloved priest-poet Jan Twardowski, who spent the last years of his life in the convent building, preached his sermons in the final years of the twentieth century. Preserved to the present day is also the historic organ on which young Chopin used to improvise. The unique ties between the composer and the Visitandines' church have been commemorated in a plaque founded in 1990 by the Chopin Society, inscribed: *In honour of Fryderyk Chopin, who played the organ in this church as a pupil of the Warsaw Lyceum in the years 1825-1826.*

The Church of the Sisters of the Visitation (the Visitandines) in a period engraving

A Church Organist at the Nuns of the Visitation

Portrait of Józef Elsner

The church organ

The Visitandines' Church – contemporary view

I have strict counterpoint with Elsner, 6 hours per week, and I attend lectures by Brodziński, Bentkowski and others, as long as they have any connection with music.

Fryderyk Chopin to Jan Białobłocki,
November, 1826

In the years 1826-29 Chopin attended the High School of Music at the Music Department of the Fine Arts and Sciences Department of the Royal University of Warsaw. Most lectures were held at the university, but for instrument practice and composition classes students would go to the Conservatory, located near the Royal Castle, on the corner of Krakowskie Przedmieście and the now non-existent Mariensztat Street. On the first floor of the building, which used to house a Cistercian convent, lived the vice-chancellor Józef Elsner, and Chopin often was a guest at his home. It was in the Conservatory concert hall that he first saw Konstancja Gładkowska, a vocal student, who would become the great love of his youth. A section of the post-Cistercian building had been adapted as a dormitory for female students, and it was there that Konstancja was living at the time she met Fryderyk. The lectures he mentions in his letter, including the ones given by dean Feliks Bentkowski, were held at the Kazimierz Palace.

The Bernardine Cistercian Nuns had occupied an old convent house since 1584. In the 17th century they moved to the new building on Krakowskie Przedmieście, between the Royal Castle and St. Anne's church, where they also ran a school for girls from noble families. After the Sisters were transferred in 1818 to Przasnysz, the building was converted into a military warehouse. In 1819 it was allocated to the Conservatory of Music (the official academic inauguration took place in April, 1821), which had had its seat there until 1831. In the 1840s the building was pulled down.

The empty square has remained thus until the present. The Mariensztat Street, which used to meet the Krakowskie Przedmieście, does not exist any more. Below the overpass runs the busy East-West crosstown motorway (Trasa W-Z), while the viewing platform in the Castle Square offers a panoramic vista of the Vistula and right-bank Warsaw.

King Sigismund's Column and Krakowskie Przedmieście Street

Student at the High School of Music

Kazimierz Palace

A view of the Castle Square

The East-West (W-Z) Motorway near the Old Town; on the far left is St. Annes' Church

In 1829 I was living in Krakowskie Przedmieście, in a tenement house on the corner of Oboźna street, and Chopin lived with his parents in the Krasiński Palace. He would come to my place three evenings a week for English lessons, which the three of us, including Julian Fontana, took from a tutor of Irish origin, quite well known in Warsaw at the time, Mr. Makartnej (McCartney)...

From Wilhelm Kolberg's memoirs

Biographers have not been able to establish the exact addresses where these lessons took place, but it is certain that Fryderyk took English in the company of Wilhelm Kolberg and Julian Fontana, while with Tytus Woyciechowski and Karol Weltz he studied Italian, also with a private tutor. In the University Library, then located in the main building of the Kazimierz Palace, he studied music scores and literature, while for knowledge in other subjects he repaired to the library of the Warsaw Society of Friends of Learning, in the Staszic Palace.

It was erected in the years 1820-1823 in the late neoclassical style, to the design by an Italian architect Antonio Corazzi. One of the founders of the project was Stanisław Staszic who wished to provide a venue for the Royal Warsaw Society of Learning. In the late 19th century the palace was turned by the ruling partitioners into a Russian Orthodox church, and it only regained its original appearance after the renovation in 1924-1926, conducted under the supervision of Marian Lalewicz. Completely destroyed during World War II, it was reconstructed by Piotr Biegański, who managed to give it back its original form; the way Corazzi had intended it.

Nowadays the Staszic Palace at 72 Nowy Świat Street is the seat of the Polish Academy of Sciences and the Warsaw Society of Learning, which coordinates exhibitions and shows commemorating important events from the city's history. In front of the building stands the monument to Copernicus by Bertel Thorvaldsen, which was unveiled on May 11, 1830, about six months before Chopin's departure from Warsaw. Stolen by the Nazis, after the war it was found near Opole and in 1945 returned to its original location.

The Copernicus monument and the Holy Cross Church

Foreign Languages and Libraries

Staszic Palace by night

The Copernicus monument in front of Staszic Palace

I go to Brzezina every day.

Fryderyk Chopin to Tytus Woyciechowski, October 3, 1829

One of Chopin's favourite pastimes was browsing through bookshelves in bookshops, and one of his favourite venues of the kind was the place in Miodowa street, owned by Antoni Brzezina, whose name he mentions in the letter. He was a regular there, bought books and sheet music, and had several of his early works printed at Brzezina's litographic workshop. Miodowa was the street for all things musical, and a few houses away there were two other shops Fryderyk liked to visit: the Karol Ludwik Magnus's store, which sold sheet music and instruments, and a similar one owned by Franciszek Klukowski. It also seems quite obvious that Chopin must have frequently popped into the bookshop in the Krasiński Palace, the very building where his parents rented the apartment at the time. He also had his favourite coffeeshops: Pani Brzezińska (Chez Mme Brzezińska), on the corner of Krakowskie Przemieście and Hoża streets, Pod Kopciuszkiem (the Cinderella) in the Tepper Palace in Miodowa, and Dziurka (the Little Hole) on the mezzanine of the same building, where he would meet with Maurycy Mochnacki, Bohdan Zaleski and Antoni E. Odyniec.

None of these venues, apart from the Krasiński Palace, exist today. The only exception is the Honoratka in the old Chodkiewicz Palace at 14 Miodowa street. Now a restaurant, it was originally established in 1826 as a coffee shop, run at the time by Mrs. Honorata Zimmermann. Besides Chopin it was frequented by Joachim Lelewel, Piotr Wysocki and Maurycy Mochancki, the patriots and conspirators who organized the November Uprising in 1830.

Chopin also spent long hours in the famous Buchholtz piano factory, located at the intersection of Mazowiecka and Świętokrzyska streets. He often tested the sound of new instruments which, thanks to his virtuoso presentation would quickly find buyers. The factory did not survive World War II, and in its place new apartment houses have been built.

The centre of contemporary Warsaw.
The intersection at Świętokrzyska and Mazowiecka Streets

Bookshops, **C**offeshops, and a **P**iano **F**actory

Telimena Coffee Shop on the corner of Kozia and Krakowskie Przedmieście Streets

The crossing of Kozia Street and Miodowa Street

Miodowa Street

For where your treasure is, there will your heart be also.

St. Matthew, 6:21, inscribed on the plaque
in the Church of the Holy Cross

The Church of the Holy Cross in Krakowskie Przedmieście Street, located in the vicinity of the three buildings where the Chopins had once made their home – the Saxon, Kazimierz and Czapski-Krasiński Palaces – was at the beginning of the nineteenth century one of the largest churches in Warsaw. Fryderyk's two sisters, Izabella and Emilia, had been baptized in that parish, and it was also there that the exequies for many great Poles, including Prince Józef Poniatowski, Stanisław Staszic, Karol Szymanowski and Leon Wyczółkowski, were held. In 1826 young Fryderyk was among the large number of mourners who came to the funeral of Stanisław Staszic. The procession lead from the Holy Cross Church to the burial place at the Immaculate Conception Church cemetery in Bielany.

The Holy Cross Church was erected in the years 1679-1696 to a Baroque design by Józef Szymon Bellloti, on the site of a church demolished during the Swedish "Deluge" invasion. The late Baroque two-towered facade was built by stages, and was finally completed in 1760 by Jakub Fontana. The most striking feature of the church is the figure, installed at the front of the steps, of Christ bearing the cross, with the inscription below reading: *Sursum corda* – Lift up your hearts. The church, reconstructed after World War II, looks the same today as it did in Chopin's times. From the original interior decor an openwork, forged metal pulpit, dated 1696, has been preserved, along with a marble baptismal font in Baroque style, and an altar – suspended in the southern arm of the transept – crafted according to the original design by Tylman of Gameren. The walls are decorated with epitaphs and plaques, commemorating, among others, Adam Mickiewicz, Juliusz Słowacki, Bolesław Prus and General Władysław Sikorski. In January of 1850 Chopin's sister Ludwika brought back to Poland an urn with her brother's heart, thus fulfilling the artist's dying wish. It was set into the second pillar on the left-hand side of the main aisle, behind a tablet bearing the composer's likeness carved by Leonardo Marconi from Carrara marble. In 1880 the Warsaw Music Society founded the plaque with the quotation from St. Matthew. In 2002 the church was raised to the distinction of a lesser cathedral, and it is from here that Polish public television Channel 1 broadcasts the Holy Mass every Sunday.

The interior of the Holy Cross Church

The Heart in the Holy Cross Church

Church of the the Holy Cross

Commemorative tablet marking the place in the wall where the urn containing the great composer's heart is interred

The Heart in Milanówek

During the Warsaw Uprising the Holy Cross Church suffered heavy damage, however, the urn containing Chopin's heart and the memorial tablet had been removed in time and hidden away. In September of 1944 it fell into the hands of the Nazi general Erich von dem Bach. He agreed to hand it over to bishop Jerzy Modzelewski of Milanówek, intending to use the event for propaganda purposes. The actual transfer took place on September 15, 1944. The urn was placed in a chapel, on the first floor of the vicarage of St. Hedwig's church in Milanówek. In 1945 Chopin's heart was returned permanently to the Holy Cross Church, as is recorded on a plaque: *17.X.1945 the heart of F. Chopin returned to Warsaw.* The urn was officially restored to its place in a solemn ceremony on the 96th anniversary of Fryderyk Chopin's death.

Some manufacturers have been experimenting with new types of instruments (...) Young Chopin either took interest in these instruments, or else was asked to give sample presentations on them. He played one such instrument during Tsar Alexander I's visit to Warsaw, and for his performance he was presented with a diamond ring.

Józef M. Chomiński, *Chopin*

In May 1825 Fryderyk performed before Tsar Alexander I during the Emperor's visit to Warsaw. The recital took place at the Augsburg Evangelical Holy Trinity Church, located on what is now Małachowski Square. Chopin played the aeolomelodicon, an instrument devised by Karol Fidelis Brunner. As a token of his appreciation the Tsar presented the young virtuoso with a diamond ring.

The church was built between 1777 and 1781 according to plans by Szymon Bogumił Zug. Shaped like a rotunda and covered with an impressive dome, it is considered the most exquisite example of early Neoclassical ecclesiastical architecture in Warsaw, evoking the Roman Pantheon in both layout and form. The interior walls are lined by two-levelled galleries, a characteristic feature of Evangelical churches. In Chopin's youth it was one of the tallest structures in Warsaw.

The church was bombed in September of 1939, and later burned down during the Warsaw Uprising, but was fully reconstructed after the war in accordance with the original design by Zug. The Holy Trinity is famous for its excellent acoustics; since it received its new German-made organ, founded by the National Augsburg Evangelical Church of Hanover, and installed in 1998, we are able to enjoy them to the fullest again.

The interior of the Holy Trinity Church

A Gift from Tsar Alexander I

The dome and organ at the Holy Trinity Church

Other Warsaw Churches

There are several other churches in Krakowskie Przedmieście and surrounding area that Chopin also attended. On days when there was no service at the Sisters Of the Visitation, his mother would take him to the Carmelite Church at 52/54 Krakowskie Przedmieście. The Bernardine Church of St. Anne at 68 Krakowskie Przedmieście was attended by Konstancja Gładkowska, and we might presume that Fryderyk also went there, if only to see her. Also, although no sources exist to confirm it, he probably attended St. John the Baptist's Cathedral in the Old Town.

Church of the Holy Trinity in Małachowski Square

...a true musical genius: not only does he perform most difficult pieces with the utmost ease and sophistication, but he is also already the author of several dances and variations of his own that music critics cannot praise highly enough.

"Pamiętnik Warszawski" (The Warsaw Diary), January 1818

This little note in a popular monthly resulted in the eight-year-old Frycek being invited to perform at the Radziwiłł Palace for the Warsaw Charitable Society on February 24, 1818. The president of the Society at the time was Julian Ursyn Niemcewicz, a statesman and an accomplished writer, and the concert was organised by the Countess Zofia Zamoyska. Fryderyk performed a piano concerto by Vojtech Jirovec, and little Zygmunt Krasiński, Chopin's junior by two years, recited poetry. It was reportedly the first public performance by the child prodigy, who was already being compared with Mozart. Frycek' s next recital took place on February 24, 1824, this time in the Society's own building, the "Res Sacra Miser" building.

The Radziwiłł Palace at No. 46/48 Krakowskie Przedmieście, also known as the Governor's, or Presidential Palace, was erected in the mid-seventeenth century for Field Marshal Stanisław Koniecpolski. In 1818, the government of the Kingdom of Poland acquired it from the Radziwiłł family and designated it as the seat of the Tsarist governor, general Józef Zajączek. The palace was then rebuilt in the Neoclassical style to a design by Chrystian Piotr Aigner. In 1821 four stone lions, the work of Camillo Landini, were placed in front of the building.

The Palace's appearance has changed many times, but it fortunately managed to escape complete destruction during World War II. After renovation in the original Neoclassical style it became the seat of the Council of Ministers, and since 1994 it has been the official residence of the President of Poland. The two wings of the building extend around to create a spacious courtyard, in which stands a statue of the mounted Prince Józef Poniatowski. A plaque on the wall of the left wing commemorates the 1791-1792 debate session of the first political party of the First Polish Republic – the Assembly of the Supporters of the Constitution of May 3, or the "Government Act" – presided over by Hugo Kołłątaj and Julian Ursyn Niemcewicz.

On the same side of the street, at 62 Krakowskie Przedmieście, stands the Neoclassical building of the Warsaw Charitable Society, the "Res Sacra Miser." It was built especially for the organisation between 1818 and 1819 according to plans by Antonio Corazzi. Reconstructed after the war, it now houses the *Caritas* Catholic Association.

Former seat of the Charitable Society, nowadays the Caritas *Catholic Association*

Concerts for the Charitable Society

Prince Józef Poniatowski monument in the courtyard of the Presidential Palace

On Sunday, a week ago today, I was at the Zamoyskis, where Długosz's aeolopantalon was admired practically the whole evening long.

Fryderyk Chopin to Jan Białobłocki, May 1826

It was not the first performance he had given at the Zamoyskis' Blue Palace at 37 Senatorska Street, as by all accounts Chopin had played there when he was just six years old. At the recital he mentions in the letter, he demonstrated a new instrument devised by Długosz's workshop. In the times of the Grand Duchy of Warsaw the Zamoyskis' was one the most fashionable society salons in town. The Charitable Society, presided over by Countess Zamoyska, organised regular musical soirees, and her famous "literary Fridays" attracted some of the most interesting people of culture, and sometimes also Russian court dignitaries. Fryderyk also performed at another salon, maintained by a popular writer and friend of the Chopins', Klementyna Tańska-Hoffmanowa, in the section of the palace facing Żabia Street.

The building, erected in the seventeenth century for Teodor Potocki, bishop of the province of Warmia, got its name from its blue-tinted roof. In 1726 King Augustus II the Strong bought the palace for his daughter Anna Orzelska and had it rebuild according to a Rococo design by Joachim Daniel Jauch. Around the mid-eighteenth century the architects Jakub Fontana and Efraim Schroeger were commissioned, the former to rebuilt and redecorate the interiors, and the latter to expand the main building. The palace then came into the possession of the Czartoryski family, and then in 1811 it was acquired by the Zamoyskis. Between 1812 and 1815 it was rebuilt again, in the then-fashionable Neoclassical style, according to designs by Fryderyk Albert Lessel. In the nineteenth century, the magnificent collection of the Zamoyski Estate Library found permanent shelter in a specially prepared pavilion there.

After the war, from 1948 to 1950, the palace was reconstructed and resumed the Neoclassical form it had had in Chopin's times. It currently houses the offices of the Municipal Board of Transportation. On the other side, directly opposite the Blue Palace, stands an original late Baroque statue of St. John Nepomucen, the work of Giovanni Liverotti from 1731.

The Blue Palace in a period litography

The Recital at the Blue Palace

Fryderyk Chopin at the piano – drawing by Eliza Radziwiłłówna

The Blue Palace – contemporary view

'The members of the Merchants' Guild, known as the Old Guild, spent yesterday's musical soiree most pleasantly (...) The singing of Mr Dorville, an artist of the French theatre, was accompanied by Mr Soliva, the listeners were then entertained by a solo performance by Mr. Bielawski, and finally by fantasies on the themes of various popular melodies performed by Mr Chopin, rounded off the evening.'

"Kurier Polski" (The Polish Courier), 20th December, 1829, No. 19

This account of the concert appeared in the press the day after the event, which took place on December 19, 1829, at the old Merchants' Guild headquarters at the Morsztyn Palace at No. 10 Miodowa Street.

The palace was built for Stanisław Morsztyn at the end of the seventeenth century. Rebuilt in the early nineteenth century in the late Neoclassical style with a design by Fryderyk A. Lessel, it was bought in 1818 by Karol Zeydler, a merchant. In the years 1820-1829 it housed the Merchants' Guild, which, after the formal split, transferred in 1829 to a building in Krakowskie Przedmieście. In the years that followed Morsztyn Palace was used as a venue for bookshops, run by Jan Glucksberg and Adam Dzwonkowski. Destroyed during the Warsaw Uprising, it was reconstructed in the 1950s in its original early eighteenth-century form. The pavilions, added by Lessel in the nineteenth century, were also rebuilt. Today the Morsztyn Palace is the seat of the PWN, the Polish Academic Publishing House.

Miodowa Street

Fantasies at the Morsztyn Palace

Morsztyn Palace

Kessler (...) gives these little musical parties. Everyone just gathers round and plays – there's no programme, everyone simply plays whatever one feels like playing at the moment.

Fryderyk Chopin to Tytus Woyciechowski,
October 20, 1829

When the news of Fryderyk's prodigious talent swept through Warsaw, invitations from some of the finest *salons* flooded in, and the young virtuoso was in constant social demand. He gave frequent performances at the salons of the Cichowskis, Duke Maksymilian Jabłonowski, the wife of General Sowiński, Teresa Kicka, Klementyna Tańska-Hoffmanowa, as well at the home of the Chopins' friends, the Wodzińskis. As a ten-year-old he is believed to have played at the home of Mrs Konstantowa Wolicka in the presence of the famous singer Angelica Catalani, who was so taken with Frycek's virtuosity that she presented him with a gold watch with an engraved dedication. Chopin also gave recitals at the home of Duchess Ludwika Czetwertyńska, and regularly appeared at Kesslers "musical Fridays," which he mentioned in his letter to Tytus Woyciechowski. Chopin was also an occasional guest at the Bruhl Palace in Wierzbowa Street, which no longer exists. He must have performed at the Potocki Palace as well, the residence of Stanisław Kostka Potocki and his wife Aleksandra, whose artistic salon was considered one of the most influential social establishments in the nineteenth-century Warsaw, however, no specific mention of this has been found in any of Chopin's correspondence.

The Potocki Palace at 15 Krakowskie Przedmieście was originally a mansion of E. Denhoff. In the mid-eighteenth century it came into the possession of the Czartoryski family, and was rebuilt in the 1760s, according to the design of Zug and Kamsetzer, acquiring two side wings. In 1799 it belonged to Stanisław Kostka Potocki and his wife Aleksandra Potocka, and thanks to their generous cultural patronage, it came to be regarded as the most influential artistic salon in Warsaw. It also went down in history as the venue of a memorable ball, given on January 22, 1807, in honour of Emperor Napoleon, during which he danced with Maria Walewska, who later became his mistress. In the nineteenth century a new pavilion was erected in the courtyard, which was later frequently used as an exhibition hall. It was there that Varsovians were able to view for the first time the two most famous patriotic canvasses by Jan Matejko, the *Battle of Grunwald (Bitwa pod Grunwaldem)*, and the *Prussian Tribute (Hołd pruski)*.

Reconstructed after the war, the palace now houses the Ministry of Culture and National Heritage. The Baroque, two-storey, rectangular building is decorated on the garden side by two oriel windows. The enclosed courtyard is entered from the street through twin Neo-Baroque gates, designed in 1897 by Henryk Marconi. The modern art gallery occupies the late Baroque guardhouse between them.

Potocki Palace by night in holiday scenery

Musical Evenings in the Salons of Warsaw

Portrait of Angelica Catalani

Around the year 1818, Chopin's "Military March," dedicated to Grand Duke Constantine, was published anonymously. Fryderyk presented it at Belvedere, and the Duke allegedly ordered to have it rewritten for the brass band and played at military parades. Since then Chopin, or rather, "little Chopin," became a popular personage about Warsaw.

Józef M. Chomiński, *Chopin*

It is not certain when exactly Fryderyk gave his first recital at Belvedere, however, according to researchers, starting in 1822 he performed there on a regular basis, at the invitation of Grand Duke Constantine and his wife, Joanna, *nee* Grudzińska.

The Baroque palace, designed in the first half of the eighteenth century by Józef Fonatana, was acquired by King Stanislaus Augustus Poniatowski and incorporated into his Royal Baths Park complex. Remodelled in the early nineteenth century in the Neoclassicist style, in 1818 it became the residence of the Russian Grand Duke Constantine. On the night of 29-30 November 1830, Belvedere became the site of a failed coup, when a group of armed conspirators and cadets from the Warsaw officers' school broke into the building and tried to kill the Duke, who, however, managed to escape, disguised in women's clothing. After Poland regained independence in 1918, the palace became the residence of the Chief of State, Józef Piłsudski and, subsequently, of all Polish presidents of the inter-war Second Polish Republic.

Fortunately, it survived World War II virtually unscathed. Located at No. 52 Belwederska Street, on the edge of the Royal Baths Park, Belvedere is now one of the official residences of the President. Inside, a permanent exhibition devoted to Józef Piłsudski is on exhibit, and in front of the palace stands a contemporary monument in his honour, designed by Jan Konarski.

Belvedere – view from the Royal Baths Park

Little Chopin at Belvedere

Belvedere – view from the Royal Baths Park; period engraving

The facade of Belvedere Palace

Flame shall devour the painted past,
Treasure'll be looted by sword-wielding thieves,
The song shall survive...

Adam Mickiewicz, *Konrad Wallenrod,* excerpt from "The prophet's song", inscribed on the base of the Chopin monument

The Royal Baths Park, where Fryderyk not only gave piano performances, but also liked to relax during his stays at Belvedere, may have been one of his childhood playgrounds, according to researchers. There he may have played with Duke Constantine's son, Paul and with Alexandrine, cleverly nicknamed "Mariolka," who was the daughter of Mikołaj Chopin's friend, a French tutor, the Count de Moriolle. It was quite a distinction for the little artist to be allowed to play there, as the Royal Baths Park were not opened to the public until the 1920s.

Considered to be the most exquisite eighteenth-century architectural garden complex in Poland, the Royal Baths Park, along with the Palace on the Water, which was once the summer retreat of the last Polish King, Stanislaus Augustus Poniatowski, became the property of Tsar Alexader I in 1817. In Chopin's youth, the complex, which included the Theatre on the Island, Old Orangerie, Little White House, and the Myślewicki Palace, made up an 80-hectare idyllic sanctuary, complete with exotic plants, fragrant flower beds and peaceful, winding paths. The park survived the turmoils of both world wars, but in one detail it varies now from the garden Chopin once knew: the Art Nouveau monument to the composer, which was unveiled in 1926.

Designed in the early twentieth century by Wacław Szymanowski, it was placed by the pond near the main entrance gate in Ujazdowskie Avenues. In 1940 the sculpture was cut up by the Nazis and removed from Warsaw. After that, the monument, which had originally depicted Chopin reclining under a willow tree, a nostalgic reference to the Mazovian landscape, was reconstructed using the preserved plaster mould and the original head, which had been discovered among the ruins of a factory in Wrocław. In 1958 the sculpture was again set on its old base in the park, but in a new setting – a concert amphitheatre designed by Oskar Sosnowski. The spot has become one of Warsaw's showcases, and one of the most identifiable symbols of the Polish capital. Since 1959, recitals of Chopin's music have been held there every Sunday, from May to late September.

The Monument in the Royal Baths Park

Palace on the Water in Royal Baths Park

A concert at the Chopin monument

The Art Nouveaux Ashtray

The Chopin monument initially was not an artistic success. The citizens of early twentieth-century Warsaw did not approve of it and openly derided it as "the Art Nouveaux ashtray." It was designed in 1908, but the casting was carried out in Paris, and the monument was not ready until the summer of 1914, when the outbreak of World War I prevented it from being installed in the park. When, on November 14, 1926, President Ignacy Mościcki finally unveiled the sculpture in Warsaw, Art Nouveaux had long been out of fashion. Today the Chopin monument is considered a masterpieces among Art Nouveau works in Poland.

Last night's concert went quite well. (...) a full house. Goerner's Symphony opened. Then I played the Allegro in E-minor, and it went so smoothly, nothing to it on the Streycher pianoforte. A roaring ovation.

Fryderyk Chopin to Tytus Woyciechowski,
October 12, 1830

Thus Fryderyk described his farewell performance of October 11, 1830 to his friend. Just six months before, on March 17, he gave his first grand public concert at the National Theatre, which he repeated five days later with the same programme. It included his own compositions, the *Concerto in F-minor*, Op. 21 and *Fantasy on Polish Airs*, Op. 13, which he performed accompanied of an orchestra directed by Karol Kurpiński. Each of the recitals was attended, according to press accounts, by eight to nine hundred people. Fryderyk knew the National Theatre, for he had often admired both Polish and foreign virtuoso performers there – from Maria Szymanowska and Niccolo Paganini, to Karol Lipiński and Henrietta Sontag.

The erection of the National Theatre in the Krasiński Square was inspired by King Stanislaus Augustus, and carried out according to Bonawentura Solari's designs in 1779. The first performance took place on September 7, 1779. Until 1833, when it was moved to a new venue on Theatre Square, the National was the largest stage in Poland. It attracted the most outstanding dramatic and musical talents of the times, thanks to the creative genius of three charismatic personalities: Wojciech Bogusławski, Józef Elsner and Karol Kurpiński, the three chief contributors to the rise and development of Polish national theatre.

Modern building of the Supreme Court

Theatre Square – on the right is Teatr Wielki (the Great Theatre), in the centre is the former Jabłonowski Palace

The Farewell Concert at the National Theatre

In 1883 the theatre building was torn down. Today, in its place stands the glass and steel edifice of the Supreme Court, and next to it rises the Monument to the Warsaw Uprising. The only building reminiscent of the old Krasiński Square is the Palace of the Republic, which used to stand opposite the National Theatre, and was reconstructed after the war in the shape originally intended by Dominik Merlini, its eighteenth-century architect. The building currently houses the National Library with its priceless collection of antique prints.

I, however, can think of nothing else except packing, for either on Saturday or Wednesday I shall be departing via Kraków.

Fryderyk Chopin to Tytus Woyciechowski,
October 12, 1830

Chopin left Warsaw on November 2, 1830, never to return to Poland again. In the letter to his friend, dated October 12, he wrote of packing for the upcoming departure. On his last day in Warsaw he had dispatched his luggage and then took a coach from the Saxon Post Office, located at the Wessles Palace in Krakowskie Przedmieście, on the corner of Kozia and Trębacka Streets. As it happened, it was not to be the location of his final farewell. Józef Elsner and a group of Conservatory students were awaiting Chopin on the outskirts of the city, at the Wola Inn. On his arrival they sang a cantata, accompanied by a guitar, composed especially for this occassion by Józef Elsner himself, entitled *Born in the Land of Poland (Zrodzony w polskiej krainie)*. The Rococo Wessel Palace, also called the Ostrowski Palace, or the Saxon Post Office, was built in the eighteenth century by the starost of Grójec, Franciszek J. Załuski. In 1761 it was acquired by the Crown's Deputy Treasurer Teodor Wessel, who in 1764 sold it to the bishop of Kujawy, Antoni Ostrowski. In 1780 it came into the possesion of Franciszek Ignacy Przebendowski, the Voivode of Pomerania and the director of the post office. From then until 1874, the building housed the Saxon Post Office. In 1882 it was remodelled according to the design of Władysław Marconi and Aleksander Woyde, gaining a third storey. At the end of the nineteenth century, two of Warsaw's most popular newspapers, "The Daily Courier" (Kurier Codzienny) and "The Illustrated Weekly" (Tygodnik Ilustrowany) were operated from the building, and in the inter-war period it was the premises of an antique shop known as the Art Palace. Burned in 1944, it was reconstructed after the war by Jan Bieńkowski according to a Rococo design which preceded the remodelling of 1882. The building at No. 25 Krakowskie Przedmieście is now the home of the Appellate Prosecutor's Office and the Judiciary Institute.

On the other hand, the suburban Wola Inn at 56 Połczyńska Street managed to survive both world wars. After World War II the building was converted into a ceramics school, and its old walls were removed from the top down to the level of the windowsills. The school was in operation until 2000, when it finally closed. Still, the plaque commemorating Chopin's final meeting with friends on his last day in Poland remains.

The old Saxon Post, today the Prosecutor's Office

The Saxon Post Office and the Wola Inn

A watercolour of a stagecoach by Piotr Michałowski, early 1830s

In Sanniki I reworked the Rondo in C-major (the latest one, if you recall) for two pianofortes, so we've tried it out today with Ernemann at Buchholtz's, and it seems to have come out rather well. We're thinking of playing it at the Guild Hall sometime.

Fryderyk Chopin to Tytus Woyciechowski, 30 September, 1828

The abundance of detail in Chopin's own correspondence, as well as the memoirs and dairies of composer's friends, makes it possible to retrace the paths of his daily routines in Warsaw, the city where he lived, relaxed, studied, performed, followed musical events in theatres and salons, met with friends in coffee shops, and visited music shops and the Buchholtz piano factory he mentions in the letter. Many of these places have been rebuilt from ruins following World War II, but, alas, for the most part, the original nineteenth-century architecture of Warsaw is simply gone.

Some of the Chopin-related sites can be located in the immediate vicinity of Krakowskie Przedmieście Street. In winter he liked to go to the skating rink on Oboźna Street; the Saxon Post Office and coach station, from where he would depart on his numerous voyages was on Kozia Street; on Miodowa Street his favourite coffee shops and bookshops posed a constant temptation. He frequently went down along Miodowa or Długa Street to get from the Krakowskie Przedmieście Street to Teatr Wielki in the Krasinski Square, and popping into their instruments shops and coffeehouses along the way. We can also map out the paths he would take to the homes of his friends and relations with some accuracy. His parents' friends apartment, the Wodzińskis, was in the same building as one of Chopin's favourite coffee shops, the *Pod Kopciuszkiem* (the Cinderella). Maurycy Mochnacki and Joachim Lelewel, with whom he often met for coffee and conversation, lived on Długa Street. He frequently took walks in the Old Town and the Saxon Square. He would take Świętojerska street to reach the New Town (Nowe Miasto), where two other friends of his lived, Alfons Brandt and Romuald Hube. He visited Józef Reinschmidt in Podwale, Antoni E. Odyniec in Senatorska, and Kajetan Koźmian on Bielańska Streets. He walked on Nowy Świat Street in the company of Marceli Celiński in the direction of the Three Crosses Square (Plac Trzech Krzyży), and would stop in to see the Pruszak family on Marszałkowska Street. Whenever Fryderyk's friend, Tytus Woyciechowski, was in town, he stayed on Miodowa Street. The friends would often walk all the way to the Piarist School in Żoliborz together, to see Leopold Poletyłło.

Krakowskie Przemieście Street

In Fryderyk's Footsteps Around Warsaw

The Castle Square as seen from Krakowskie Przedmieście Street

The Church of the Holy Cross on Krakowskie Przedmieście Street

The final resting place of all of Chopin's closest family members is Powązki Cemetery, established in 1790, and according to accounts of those who knew him, he also wished to be buried there. Fryderyk's sister Emilia, who died of consumption in 1827, was the first member of the family to be laid to rest in Powązki. The eldest sister, Ludwika Jędrzejewiczowa, was buried in 1855 in the Jędrzejewicz family grave (plot 175-II-6/7), to which Emilia's ashes were also eventually transferred. The remains of Mikołaj Chopin, who passed away in 1844, and his wife Justyna, nee Krzyżanowska, who died in 1861, were interred in the catacombs until 1948, and afterwards they were transferred to plot 9-IV-1, next to the grave of Stanisław Moniuszko. The last to pass away was Chopin's youngest sister Izabella Barcińska, who rests in the family grave of the Barcińskis in plot II-II-9/10. Fryderyk's teachers are also buried in Powązki – Wojciech Żywny (plot 12-II-20) and Józef Elsner (plot 159-V-1), whose tomb is adorned with a statue of the Weeping Muse.

The tomb of Chopin's parents

The Family Graves in the Powązki Cemetery

The tomb of the Jędrzejewicz family, where the ashes of Emilka Chopin are interred

The tomb of the Barciński family where Chopin's sister – Izabella Barcińska

The tomb of Józef Elsner

The tomb of Wojciech Żywny

Call forth: "Rejoice, late-coming posterity!
The vulgar street – screech muted stones –
The Ideal – has inherited."

Cyprian Kamil Norwid, *Chopin's Grand Piano,*
translated by Teresa Bałuk, 2000:13

The palace of Count Andrzej Artur Zamoyski at No. 67/69 Nowy Świat Street acquired its present appearance long after Chopin left for Paris. During the January Insurrection of 1863 it became the site of an incident that inspired Cyprian Kamil Norwid to write his most famous poem, from which comes the stanza quoted above.

The history of the palace goes back to late seventeenth century, when it was the property of Jan Wielopolski. In the eighteenth century it was remodelled under the supervision of Szymon Bogumił Zug. When in 1802 it came under the ownership of Anna Sapieżyna, nee Zamoyska, Stanisław Staszic lived there, and continued to until his death in 1826. This Neoclassical building was what Chopin would have known, if only by sight, as the Zamoyski Palace. Between 1834 and 1846 Count Andrzej A. Zamoyski commisioned Henryk Marconi to renovate the palace, which he did in the Neo-Renaissance fashion, and for a more striking effect had sculptures of mythological scenes by Paweł Maliński added to the tympanum. When Chopin's sister, Izabella Barcińska, and her husband moved into the palace's first floor apartment in 1855, she brought with her numerous family mementoes and possessions, including Fryderyk's old pianoforte.

On the evening of September 19, 1863, when the Governor of the Kingdom of Poland, General Fyodor Berg was returning along Nowy Świat Street to his quarters in the Royal Castle, an attempt was made on his life by members of the National Guard from the attic windows of the Zamoyski Palace. Several bombs were hurled at his carriage. The attempt failed, and the general was unhurt, but his aide-de-camp and several of the entourage's horses suffered injuries. In retribution, the Russian army brutally evicted the innocent Stanisław Antoni Zamoyski, Count Andrzej's son, from his gabled flat. The palace was confiscated, and Andrzej Zamoyski fled to France, while his son Stanisław was imprisoned in the Warsaw Citadel and subsequently sentenced to eight years of hard labour. During the furious search, the Tsarist troops plundered and vandalised the palace, tossing books and manuscripts out the windows, along with Chopin's sheet music, valuable paintings and smashed furniture, and then burned it all at the foot of the Copernicus monument below. Chopin's pianoforte, the one he used to play in his home, was also thrown from a window, and fell crashing to the ground. The national heritage of Poland had suffered an irretrievable loss.

In 1867 the Zamoyski palace became the headquarters of the Warsaw District War Engineering Command, and in the inter-war period it was the seat of the Ministry of Internal Affairs. During the Siege of Warsaw in 1939 it housed the Warsaw Defence Command, which is commemorated by a historical plaque. Destroyed during the Warsaw Uprising, it was rebuilt in the years 1948-1950. Today it houses a number of departments and institutes of the University.

The Grand Piano from the Zamoyski Palace

Zamoyski Palace in Nowy Świat Street

...in the vaults of the old castle lives an cursed princess in the form of a golden duck.

Artur Oppman, *The Warsaw Legends*

According to the legend, in the catacombs stretching underneath the Gniński-Ostrogski Palace, lived a golden duck who guarded a great treasure. In the early nineteenth century, Fryderyk Chopin would have seen the crumbling building. Today the palace at Tamka Street (entrance at 1 Okólnik Street) houses the Chopin Museum, and the building next to it is home to the Chopin Centre.

The palace was erected in the years 1681-1685 according to the plans of Tylman of Gameren. After renovation in 1859 it was transferred to the Warsaw Conservatory. When World War II ended, it was rebuilt to match the original design and designated the Fryderyk Chopin Society and Museum. To celebrate the bicentennial anniversary of the Master's birth in 2010, the palace has been thoroughly refurbished, and the museum gained additional exposition space and new exhibits, while in the adjacent square a modern Chopin Centre has been built, to accommodate the Fryderyk Chopin Institute, a library, a collection of recordings, conference facilities, and a tourist centre.

The Chopin Centre

The museum boasts an impressive collection – over seven thousand items of Chopin memorabilia: letters, portraits, autographs, and also the piano on which he worked for the last two years of his life. Among the most valuable new acquisitions are the original manuscripts of *Tarantella*, Op. 43, and *Etude in F-Minor*, as well as the diary of the Baroness d'Este. Modern audio-visual technology makes it possible for the visitors to be transported to the places closest to Chopin's heart – Żelazowa Wola, his favourite places in Warsaw, and the salons of Paris. The yellowed pages of the Master's letters are not only available for viewing, but we can also hear them read aloud by some of our most talented actors. Just looking at Chopin's last pianoforte, we can recreate the atmosphere of the Parisian salons in our imaginations, and even hear some of the everyday sounds of the city: hum of conversations in the streets, the shouts of newspaper vendors, or street hawkers peddling their wares.

As for the mysterious vaults underneath the palace, where the infamous golden duck once dwelt, they have now been converted into a spacious concert hall.

The Chopin Museum and Centre

A portrait plaque made in 1926 by Józef Aumiler

Former Ostrogski palace nowadays houses the Chopin Museum

The National Philharmonic Hall, on the corner of Jasna, Moniuszki and Sienkiewicza Streets, is a venue familiar to music lovers from all over the world, because it is here that International Fryderyk Chopin Piano Competition is held every five years. The building, designed by Karol Kozłowski and Izydor Pianka, was erected for the Warsaw Philharmonic between 1900 and 1901. The sculptures on the facade are the work of Stanisław R. Lewandowski and Władysław Mazur, and ceiling in the concert hall was painted by Henryk Siemiradzki. The eclectic interior decor was inspired by similar European venues of the times. Destroyed during the Warsaw Uprising and rebuilt in the Neoclassical style, it was reopened on February 21, 1955, to inaugurate the Fifth International Fryderyk Chopin Piano Competition.

The National Philharmonic Hall

The grand piano at the Warsaw Philharmonic

The National Philharmonic Hall in Warsaw

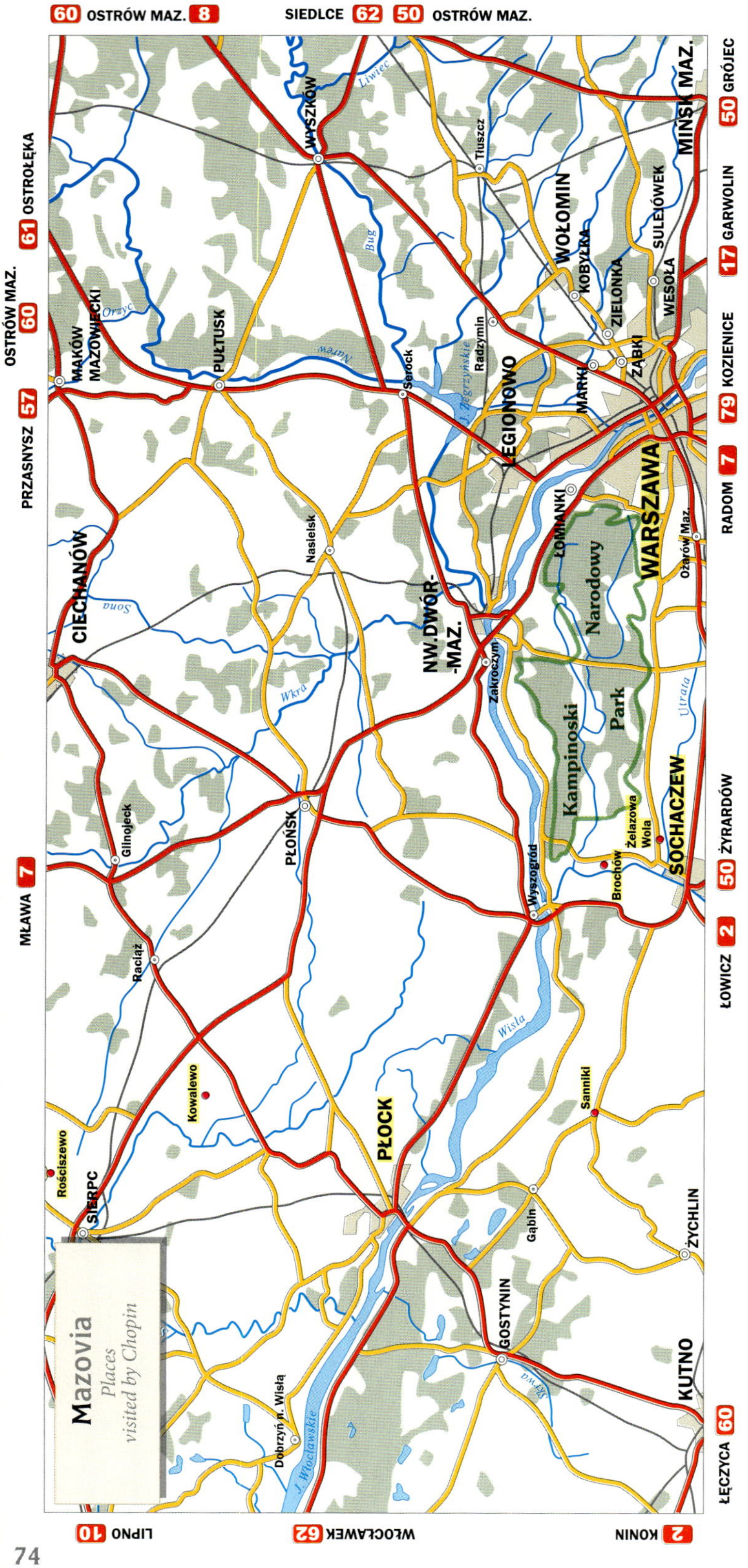
Mazovia
Places visited by Chopin
60 OSTRÓW MAZ. 8
SIEDLCE 62
50 OSTRÓW MAZ.
GRÓJEC 50
GARWOLIN 17
KOZIENICE 79
RADOM 7
ŻYRARDÓW 50
ŁOWICZ 2
ŁĘCZYCA 60
KONIN 2
WŁOCŁAWEK 62
LIPNO 10
MŁAWA 7
PRZASNYSZ 57
OSTRÓW MAZ. 60
OSTROŁĘKA 61
WYSZKÓW
Tłuszcz
WOŁOMIN
KOBYŁKA
ZIELONKA
SULEJÓWEK
WESOŁA
MIŃSK MAZ.
Radzymin
MARKI
ZĄBKI
LEGIONOWO
Serock
PUŁTUSK
MAKÓW MAZOWIECKI
CIECHANÓW
Nasielsk
NW.DWÓR-MAZ.
ŁOMIANKI
WARSZAWA
Ożarów Maz.
Kampinoski Park Narodowy
Zakroczym
SOCHACZEW
Żelazowa Wola
Brochów
Wyszogród
PŁOŃSK
Glinojeck
Raciąż
Kowalewo
Rościszewo
SIERPC
PŁOCK
Sanniki
Gąbin
ŻYCHLIN
GOSTYNIN
KUTNO
Dobrzyń n. Wisłą
Bug
Narew
Liwiec
Orzyc
Sona
Wkra
Wisła
Utrata
J. Zegrzyńskie
J. Włocławskie
Skrwa

Mazovia

Żelazowa Wola

You will never guess where I am writing from!...(...) Don't even waste your time trying, for I'm in Żelazowa Wola (...), have just got out of the buggy, and am about to sit down to Christmas Eve supper. Clearly, Fate must have ordained it, for Mother was adamantly against it and wouldn't hear of us going, but it couldn't be helped, and here we are, Ludwika and I, in Żelazowa Wola.

Fryderyk Chopin to Jan Białobłocki, Christmas Eve, 1825

Except for during his infancy, Chopin never actually lived in Żelazowa Wola. However, the Skarbek family house was always a kind of second home to him. As a schoolboy and student would visit during religious holidays, and spent joyous summers there. He said his final farewell to that place in the last days of the summer of 1830, before leaving his homeland forever.

The village lies on the edge of the Kampinos Forest, 54 kilometres west of Warsaw; it can even be reached from the nearby Sochaczew on foot, walking along a historic avenue. The name of the estate comes from its sixteenth-century landowners, Mikołaj and Piotr Żelazo. At the turn of the eighteenth century it was acquired by Kacper and Ludwika Skarbek. Shortly afterwards, Count Skarbek, deep in debt, fled abroad – leaving his wife to take care of the estate and the family. In 1802 the Countess employed a French-born tutor, Mikołaj Chopin, to oversee the education of her son Fryderyk, who was later to become a writer and economist. It was there that Mikołaj met the Skarbeks' cousin, Tekla Justyna Krzyżanowska, who was the housekeeper there. They were married and moved into the annex on the left wing of the manor house. A year later the Chopins' eldest daughter, Ludwika, was born, and on March 1, 1810 – their only son.

Portraits of Chopin's parents

The Chopin family left Żelazowa Wola in October of 1810, but their relationship with the Countess and her five children did not fade. Despite the difference in social status, the two families, though only distantly related, were united by a genuinely affectionate friendship. They visited and supported one another in difficult times. Michał Skarbek, who later became the master of the estate, would borrow money from Mikołaj Chopin when he found himself in financial troubles. During Fryderyk's visits to Żelazowa Wola much of their time was spent playing music. In the summer the piano was removed to the garden, and the young composer would give improvised recitals under the chestnut trees. His audience extended beyond family and friends – those performances would live in the memories of the villagers, hearing the music as it carried over their fences.

During his visits, Chopin probably stayed in his parents' old quarters in the left annex. Now grandly referred to as the "manor house," at the time it was really a very modest building, reflecting the status of its tenants.

In 1834 the indebted Michał Skarbek committed suicide, and the village, along with the mansion and farm buildings, changed hands. From 1859 to 1879 the owner of the estate was Adam Towiański, son of Andrzej Towiański at the time a well known but controversial philosopher and mystic. He wished to preserve the composer's birthplace, and sought to remodel the "Chopin" annex and add a porch. Unfortunately, in 1879 the estate came into the possession of one Aleksander Pawłowski, a more pragmatic fellow, who used the building as a storage shed. It was not until the Russian composer and lover of Chopin's music, Mily Balakirev, having taken the trouble of travelling to Żelazowa Wola and assessing the condition of the house, brought to public attention the lamentable state of the site. It was his initiative that made possible the first monument to Chopin, unveiled in 1894 in Żelazowa Wola – an obelisk with a medallion, depicting Chopin with a lyre, and bearing the simple inscription: *F. Chopin 22.II.1810.*

Portrait of Ludwika Chopin, Fryderyk's eldest sister

Portrait of Izabella Chopin

Portrait of the youngest sister, Emilka

During the First World War, most of the estate buildings were destroyed by fire, and in 1918 the land was divided up among the local peasants. The preserved Chopin annex along with the old park became the property of Roch Szymaniak, who cut down most of the trees. It was only in 1926 that, through the diligent work of the newly established Society for the Friends of Chopin's Home and the Chopin Committee from Sochaczew, it became possible to collect the necessary 40 thousand zlotys to purchase the annex along with the ravaged park. Thanks to public support, numerous antique objects and pieces of period furniture, including a Pleyel grand piano, were donated to the budding museum, and the surroundings were beautified with exotic shrubs and trees. Thus renovated "manor" was officially opened to visitors on October 17, 1931. After World War II the reconstruction had to be repeated, as the exhibits had been stolen and the garden ruined beyond recognition.

In 1953 the Warsaw Fryderyk Chopin Society became the guardian of the estate, and in 2005 this function was taken over by the National Fryderyk Chopin Institute, which has owned the site since 2009. In preparations for the upcoming Year of Chopin, the park in Żelazowa Wola has been extended and refurbished, and a new information centre has been established.

The Skarbek manor house in Żelazowa Wola in a nineteenth-century engraving

The interior of the manor house in Żelazowa Wola

In one of the rooms stands a period piano called the "Wrocław Giraffe"

One of Chopin monuments in front of the Żelazowa Wola manor

The present layout of the house – a hallway dividing the house along its long axis with the fireplace room (previously a kitchen), dining room and music room on the right, and the mother's room, children's room and father's study on the left – is just a matter of convention. The intention was to recreate the atmosphere of an early nineteenth-century manor house. In the mother's room, a marble vase with fresh-cut flowers symbolically marks Fryderyk's hypothetical place of birth. The interior has been furnished with Biedermeier-style furniture and instruments of the period, such as the piano by Warsaw's Leszczyński and the nineteenth-century upright piano, nicknamed "the Wrocław giraffe," but there is also a modern grand piano. The tiled stove and the ceilings, decorated with wooden beams and painted plant motifs, are the two features preserved from the original decor. Replicas of portraits of the members of Chopin's family hang on the walls and facsimiles of his documents and manuscripts, such as music scores and letters, are on exhibit.

In 1954 the pianist and teacher Zbigniew Drzewiecki started an initiative for a summer Chopin concert series, and over the years the performances have become an annual tradition in Żelazowa Wola. Recently, an exciting new project entitled *Musical Presentations* has begun showcasing talented young pianists. The artist plays indoors in front of open windows and the audience listens from outside in the picturesque park, reconstructed in 1930s. The park contains over 10 thousand specimens of shrubs, plants and trees, including California pines and the thorny flowering quince from China. There are several monuments to the composer in Żelazowa Wola: the obelisk on the edge of the park, a sandstone bust of Chopin made by Stanisław Sikora (1968), a bronze statue by Józef Gosławski, unveiled on the one hundred and twentieth anniversary of Chopin's death (1969), and Zofia Wolska's bronze bust on a sandstone base, funded by the Stadtmuseum in Düsseldorf.

Brochów

In the year eighteen hundred and ten, on the twenty-third day of the month of April, in the third hour of the afternoon, stood before us, the undersigned pastor of Brochów, empowered with the authority of the civil servant of the community of Brochów of the county of Sochaczew in the district of Warsaw, Mikołaj Chopin (...) and presented to us his child, of the male gender, who was born in his house on the twenty-second day of the month of February, at six o'clock in the evening, of this year (...)

Entry in the parish book of records

All of the Chopin family birth certificates are preserved in the parish archives. However, the date of February 22, entered as the date of Fryderyk's birth is considered to be an error ... made by the church organist. Fryderyk always celebrated his birthday on March first, as did his whole family, recalling the day when Mikołaj Chopin, played the violin to ease his nerves while anxiously awaiting the outcome of the labour.

The baby was named after his godfather, Count Fryderyk Skarbek, who was not, however, able to attend the christening. The baby was held on his behalf by Franciszek Grębecki – hence Fryderyk's middle name, Franciszek. However, some sources claim he could have been given his middle name after his grandfather. The count's daughter, Anna Skarbkówna was the godmother. The ceremony took place on April 23, 1810, at the same church where Fryderyk's parents were married. It was there also that, years later, in 1832, Fryderyk's sister Ludwika was to exchange wedding vows with Józef Jędrzejewicz.

The Brochów church of St. Roch and St. John the Baptist is not an unassuming country church – it is an impressive Gothic-Renaissance edifice, which once served both religious and defensive functions. The village of Brochów had been attacked and razed so many times over the course of its history (during the Swedish Deluge, the Napoleonic Wars, and then again in 1915) that the martial appearance of the church (three cylindrical towers, a tunnelled gallery equipped with shooting loopholes) seems only too well justified. Funded by Jan Brochowski, it was built of red brick in 1551-1596 by Jan Baptysta Wenecjanin. In the seventeenth century it was surrounded with a moat and a defensive wall. During the battle of Bzura in 1939, the Polish army used one of the church towers as an observation point. The three-nave basilica, with its polychromed barrel vault, is known for its excellent acoustics. In the summer, Chopin recitals are held there and visitors can also often hear a Chopin composition performed on the church organ. The direct route connecting Brochów with Żelazowa Wola is 8 km long and is currently under construction, but is projected to be completed in time for the Year of Chopin. At present, the most convenient but longer route runs through Sochaczew.

The church in Brochów

Sochaczew

The other day I visited Gen. Szembek's camp again. You should know he's always garrisoned in Sochaczew, and he'd arranged for Michał to drive me to him. When that plan failed, he sent Czajkowski's aide – you know Czajkowski, he's the brother of that Miss Czajkowska, the one who plays and then faints – to bring me to him…

Fryderyk Chopin to Tytus Woyciechowski

General Piotr Szembek loved music, and was himself an accomplished violinist – his showpieces were Paganini compositions – but his true passion was his regimental orchestra. On August 29, 1830, he invited Chopin into his camp in Sochaczew, to play together at an impromptu musical party. The camp was located in the disused quarters of a Dominican convent (near the ruins of the Mazovian Princes' castle), which were allocated to the military after the dissolution of the nunnery. Although Chopin and the General promised to repeat their evening together, they never did. Two months later Chopin left Poland forever, and one month after that General Szembek and his Third Infantry Brigade lit out from Sochaczew to support the November Insurrection. That event was commemorated by the poet Antoni Bogusławski: *Out of Sochaczew, wading in mud / that like a river has flooded / March on eagerly, arm in arm, / the soldiers of Szembek's Brigade.*

Fryderyk described the spontaneous musical evening at the garrison in a letter: *he is very musical and plays the violin well (…) and he is a rabid Paganinist, which places him in the right company. (…) He has a pianoforte at the camp, and I don't know how, but, in God's name, he truly did see my meaning…*

Chopin must have known Sochaczew well from other occasions. He would pass through on summer trips to Szafarnia, and stop over there with Michał Skarbek during his holidays in Żelazowa Wola. The Fryderyk Chopin Music School in the nearby village of Czerwonka, located in the Garbolewski family manor house which organises concerts and competitions for young musicians. Students of the school also give recitals in Żelazowa Wola. In 1961 a Chopin obelisk was unveiled in Sochaczew, at the intersection of Warszawska and Traugutta Streets, with an inscription: *Fryderyk Chopin 1810-1849.* It should also be born in mind that it was the community of Sochaczew, outraged at the deteriorating condition of the composer's birthplace, that had established the Chopin Committee, with the intention of buying out Żelazowa Wola. Today the old Committee offices house the Local Tourist Organisation "Mazowsze Chopina" (Chopin's Mazovia). And Sochaczew's own pastry shop, "Lukrecja" expect their new sweet temptations, their "Chopin's Mazurkas," to be a special hit this year.

A landscape in Sochaczew

Sanniki

In Sanniki I reworked the Rondo in C-major (the latest one, if you recall) for two pianofortes, so we've tried it out today with Ernemann at Buchholtz's, and it seems to have come out rather well.

Fryderyk Chopin to Tytus Woyciechowski, 30 September, 1828

Fryderyk spent the summer of 1828 in Sanniki, in the comfortable, spacious manor of Konstanty Pruszak, his school friend, whose parents were very wealthy people. He had a wonderful time playing with Kostek and his younger sister, strolling about the extensive park grounds, shaded by ancient trees, playing music together and taking day trips in the area. Soon after his return to Warsaw, a new, exiting opportunity opened up before Fryderyk – a journey to Berlin. It's hardly surprising that that news predominated in his letters to Tytus Woyciechowski, and that he hardly mentions Sanniki. Besides, there was no real need to describe for him either the place, nor his hosts: *I was staying at the Pruszaks' at the time. I spent the whole summer there. – I'm not going to bore you with details of our games and schemes, since you know Sanniki, having been there yourself.*

Konstanty Pruszak, the son of one of the wealthiest landowners in Mazovia, was a student at the Warsaw Lyceum, like Fryderyk. When his parents were away enjoying their country home, he would stay with the Chopins. The Pruszaks repaid this hospitality by inviting Fryderyk to their splendid Warsaw home, whose doors were always open to all of their son's friends. The boys were invited to Sunday dinners, where they staged plays, in which Konstanty's younger sister, Weronika always wanted to star. The girl, called "Olesia" by friends and family, also took piano lessons from Fryderyk. He tutored her without enthusiasm, but was always writing about her to Tytus Woyciechowski – trying to make a match of his two friends. Then an unfortunate incident occurred: Fryderyk himself was accused of seducing Olesia's governess, and rumour had it that he was the father of her unborn child. The misunderstanding was soon cleared up, and consequently Fryderyk became godfather to the illegitimate child.

Sanniki is a village situated about 30 km northwest of Sochaczew. In the middle ages, along with other settlements and villages of the area, it was the property of the Princes of Płock. The earliest existing description of the mansion – then a wooden building, its pitched roof broken, and surrounded by a garden with a linden-lined avenue – dates from January 16, 1775. Aleksander Pruszak, Konstanty's father, inherited the estate from his uncle and expanded both the house and the park. The old wooden manor no longer stands; the Neoclassical mansion which can be admired in its place today was built according to the plans of Władysław Marconi, in 1910 for the subsequent owners of the estate, Antonina and Stefan Dziewulski. Only the old trees in the park now recall the three friends playing there: Frycek, Kostek and Olesia.

In 1981 the Fryderyk Chopin Memorial Centre was established in the left wing of the estate complex, with a concert hall and a small museum, and 1985 a monument to Chopin, the work of Ludwika Nitschowa, was placed in front of the palace. The statue is of a man wrapped in an overcoat with a melancholy expression, not at all reminiscent of the bright, vibrant youth who once ran through the old park. A year later, the Mateusz Gliński Music Library was established on the first floor of the palace, with a collection of works about the life and music of Fryderyk Chopin. The Centre is also actively involved in local folk culture, and every June the mansion grounds become the scene of the Sanniki Sunday, a regional folk festival. From February to October the Sunday concerts with reading of Polish poetry are held in the palace, and in those two months the events are always set on the Sundays closest to the dates marking the anniversaries of Chopin's birth and death.

The interior of the palace in Sanniki – today the Chopin Commemorative Centre

The Sanniki park, although replanted and redesigned many times, still boasts splendid botanical specimens, some of which, like the chestnut-lined avenue leading to the palace from the Sochaczew-Gąbin crossroads, and the row of linden trees, mentioned in the 1775 description, would have an anecdote or two to tell about the 18-year-old Fryderyk, if only they could speak. Chopin's stay is commemorated by a plaque, placed on the front wall of the building in 1925.

The Sanniki Palace is currently undergoing extensive renovations and will not be open to visitors until the end of 2010.

Chopin monument in Sanniki park

The Sanniki palace

The Płock Region

It is morning now, 8 o'clock (...), the air is fresh, the sun is shining, the birds are chirping, there's no stream, or else I'd hear it burbling, but there's a pond, and the frogs are singing beautifully...

From Fryderyk Chopin's letter written in Kowalewo to his parents in Warsaw

In the summer of 1827 Fryderyk Chopin travelled a great deal; on his way to Pomerania he stopped for the night at the hospitable residence of some friends, and then, after leaving for the next destination, checked in at the post office in Płock for letters from his parents. *So, today in Płock, tomorrow Rościszewo, the day after Kikół, then for a few days to Turzno, and a couple in Kozłów, then quickly off to Gdańsk, and back home again,* he outlines the hectic itinerary of his trip in the letter written at the manor house of Count Ksawery Zboiński (the godfather of Emilia Chopin) in Kowalewo.

Płock. Tumskie Hill

At the time the Zboińskis had three small children. In one of the letters to his parents Fryderyk writes: *While the blackbird outside my window is the funniest thing of all, their littlest one, Kamila, is just as funny; she's not two yet, but seems to like me and keeps babbling, "Kalila lufs you"...*

The Zboiński manor house, where Fryderyk stopped on his way to Gdańsk, does not exist anymore. The building which today stands – barely, as its dilapidated condition requires immediate repairs – was built in its place 1859, for the next owner of Kowalewo, Antoni Jabłoński. The hamlet lies 4 km from the town of Drobin, the seat of the local government, which now owns the property.

The church in Kowalewo

A road near Kowalewo

Płock

From Kowalewo Fryderyk travelled to Płock to pick up his letters. Count Zboiński, who rode with Fryderyk, wouldn't miss a chance to visit the old Mazovian town and took his guest on a sightseeing tour. He must have been a knowledgeable guide, but it hard to say what exactly Fryderyk saw during this short visit, or how it affected him, as nothing is known of his impressions of the place.

We shall presume, then, that he visited the cathedral on the Tumskie hill, with its tombs of Polish Kings and Mazovian Princes. The oldest church in Płock, it was erected on the high right bank of the River Vistula (the whole town was on that side at the time) in the eleventh century. In Chopin's times, however, it looked quite different than it does today, due to renovations carried out between 1784 and 1787 by Bishop Michał Poniatowski. His main objective at the time was to save the facade, which was in danger of collapsing; it was secured with a thick wall and decorated with heavy, corniced attics resting on Ionic pillars. The massive, Neoclassical portico clashed with the original design and met with public criticism. The previous renovation (1531-1534), however, carried out in the Renaissance style, drew praise for the church as the first north of the Alps to have been laid out according to Leonardo Da Vinci's rules of design. In Chopin's times the pride of the cathedral was the newly opened Royal Chapel. In 1825 the remains of the Piast dynasty Kings Ladislaus Herman and Boleslaus III the Wry-mouthed, along with 15 Mazovian Princes were discovered under the chancel floor and transferred to a separate crypt located under the northern tower, and finally covered with a black marble sarcophagus. Ornamented with an alabaster eagle and golden crown insignia, it bears the inscription: *Rulers and heirs to the lands of: Cracovia, Sandomiria, Silesia, Greater Poland, Mazovia, Dobrin, Michałów, Łęczyca and Pomerania.* Chopin probably kneeled before the altar, which is carved from coloured marble and devoted to Our Lady of Mazovia, who is venerated as the patron saint of the region. The cathedral's greatest treasures were at that time – and still are – the thirteenth-century chalice, founded by Prince Conrad of Mazovia, and the St. Sigismund vacuum reliquary, founded in fourteenth century by King Casimir III the Great, and adorned with a golden thirteenth-century crown. Chopin could not have seen, alas, the famous Płock Doors, as the ones we are able to admire today (they separate the main aisle from the porch) are 1980s replicas of the twelfth-century original. The doors, decorated in 24 sections depicting biblical scenes, were commissioned in Magdeburg by the Bishop of Płock. Probably looted by Lithuanians by the thirteenth century, they were taken to Veliky Novgorod, Russia, where remain today.

The cathedral basilica, as we know it today, restored to its Renaissance form, its Romanesque elements uncovered and its rich polychrome renovated, is the glorious result of reconstruction conducted at the outset of the twentieth century by Stefan Szyller. The main altar is quite new – it was added in 2003, but the side altars, old epitaphs and tombs are original.

During the walk around Płock Chopin could not have missed the old castle of Polish Kings and Mazovian Princes – or, rather its two surviving Gothic towers, rising up near the cathedral. The Nobles' Tower (from the thirteenth century) was shortened in the eighteenth century, before which it was know as the High Tower), but the Clock Tower (fifteenth-century, now the cathedral belfry) was left unchanged. In the sixteenth century, a section of the castle's defensive wall and the slope on which it was standing was destroyed in a landslide; the remaining buildings were taken over by Benedictine monks, who rebuilt them as a Baroque abbey. At the time of Chopin's visit it housed a seminary.

The River Vistula and Tumskie Hill in Płock

In the centre of Płock, Zboiński could have shown Fryderyk the then brand-new Classicist town hall, which had just been erected in 1827 by Jakub Kubicki. The two visitors could not have possibly known that this representative building would become, in four years' time, the site of the last session of the Assembly of the November Insurrection, where the decision would be taken to dissolve the rebel forces and to emigrate. Today the town hall is the seat of the city government, and the Old Market, now adorned with a fountain, is the showpiece of the city.

Płock City Hall

The beautifully lit towers of the Płock Cathedral

The interior of the Płock Cathedral

Rościszewo

Fryderyk Chopin and Count Zboiński made several other stops on their journey to Pomerania. Their road wound through Rościszewo, situated on the River Skrwa Prawa valley (10 km north of Sierpc), where they stayed at the hospitable abode of the Jeżewski family. We know that the company attended Sunday mass at the local Church of the Care of St. Joseph. It was founded by general Benedykt Jeżewski and built during the years 1779-1781, in the Baroque style. It has since retained its original character and its historic pulpit is worth a look.

The Jeżewskis' two-annex manor house, erected at the end of the eighteenth century by Benedykt Jeżewski, and since then rebuilt twice, is still standing. The entire estate, situated in the heart of the hamlet, stretches over about 2 hectares of land, including the park grounds.

The manor house was renovated and converted into a culture centre, complete with a library and a memorial chamber dedicated to Fryderyk Chopin. Above the entrance gate there is an inscription: *Chopin's Rościszewo is the centre of Polishness. Here a man can drink in and breathe in the Motherland.*

The ceremonial blessing of the site was held 180 years after Fryderyk's visit. The event was accompanied by a recital of Chopin's music, and pupils of the local schools performed in a spoken word and musical presentation entitled "Just like Soplicowo" about the composer's stay with the Jeżewski family. The event served as the basis for the program *Encounters with Chopin's Music in Rościszewo*, now a local tradition.

The church in Rościszewo

Rościszewo – former manor house of the Jeżewski family

Dobrzyń and Chełmno Regions

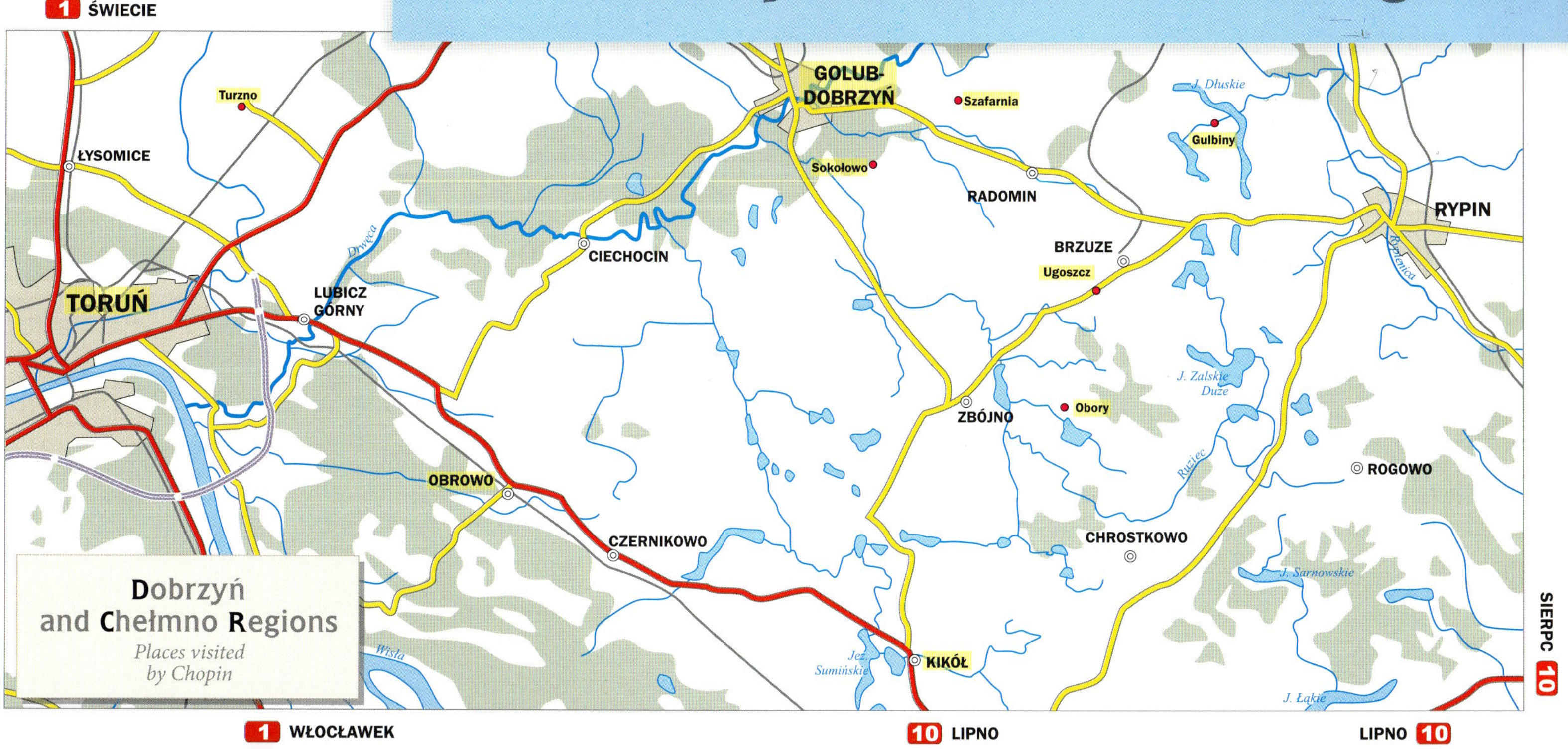

Szafarnia

That day there were harvest festivals of two villages taking place. There we were, sitting at supper, finishing up the last course, when suddenly from a distance a chorus of out-of-tune sounds, sung at one moment by women, honking through their noses, then by girls, half a tone higher, and squeaking unmercifully with the larger part of their faces, was heard, accompanied by a single violin with only three strings, which sounded its alto voice every time a couplet ended (…). Having abandoned the company at the table, Domuś and I ran out into the garden, where a whole crowd, coming step by slow step steadily approached the house.

Excerpt from Fryderyk's letter to his parents from Szafarnia

At the end of July 1824, the fourteen-year-old Fryderyk, having completed the fourth form at the Warsaw Lyceum, travelled to the family estate of his schoolmate and friend, Dominik Dziewanowski, or "Domuś," in Szafarnia, where he spent that and the following summer in the village, 7 kilometres distance from Golub-Dobrzyń. They were as truly country holidays as could be imagined, full of new experiences and constant amusement. Fryderyk spent time playing with Domuś, eagerly participated in the social life of the family, who, having been settled in Szafarnia for many years, had long-established friendly relations with the other landowners of the area. He took walks and horseback rides, rode around the adjacent villages, and edited the *Kuryer Szafarski* (Szafarnia Courier) – a humorous paper, whose editor-in-chief was a Mr Pichon (an anagram of "Chopin"), and the censor was Dominik's sister, Ludwika, with whom he also played four-handed pieces on the piano. *"Chopin was interested in everything, whether it was the servants' fighting, the frolics of the household animals, or the peasants or Jewish renters going about their own business,"* writes Adam Zamoyski in his biography of Chopin, *"but what fascinated him more than anything else was the world of folk music. He would listen to young peasant girls sing their songs of love and grief, to old women wailing while at work in the fields, and to the drunken songs coming from the inn. At the end of August, Fryderyk and company set off for a nearby village for the harvest festival, where he watched the peasants dancing mazurkas late into the night."*

His two stays in Szafarnia, according to researchers, had a profound impact on Chopin's artistic sensibilities, and the improvised mazurkas he played at the Dziewanowski's home, based on themes he had heard in folk songs there, were to become the precursors to his later mature works as a composer.

Szafarnia lies within the former Sokołowski Forest, once overgrown with pines and oaks. Near the larch wood manor house of the Dziewanowski family, the forest gradually changed into a park, adjacent to a vegetable garden, the orchards and two small ponds. The old house was, however, demolished in 1910 by its new owner, who erected a small eclectic palace in its place.

A Chopin bust in front of the Szafarnia manor house

Piątek
Dnia 27 Sierpnia 1824
KURYER SZAFARSKI.
Wiadomości Krajowe. —
Wspomnienie.
Wiadomości zagraniczne. —
Wolno pozwolić Cenzor L. D.

A page from "Kuryer Szafarski" ("The Szafarnia Courier")

Szafarnia, now a part of Radomin Community in the Golub-Dobrzyń county, remains the small village Chopin once knew. The renovated little palace houses the Chopin Centre, with a concert chamber and a small museum. In front of the building stands a bust of the composer, and to its right is a small annex, which would probably remember Chopin's visit. The Centre is surrounded by a 3-hectare landscape park, with some impressive natural monuments, such as the Chopin Linden Tree and the Dziewanowskis' Oaks; there is also a pond, designed in the shape of a fortepiano, while that intention may not be immediately recognised by a viewer today.

In the nearby hamlet of Płonne, once a part of the Dziewanowski estate, the old manor park and the Gothic church from the turn of the fourteenth century have been preserved, together with the obelisk in memory of the war hero Jan Dziewanowski (1782-1808), known as "the fearless knight," commander of Napoleon's Third Company of the 1st Regiment of the Light Cavalry of the Guard, who was killed in the victorious charge at Somosierra canyon in Spain. On another note, writer Maria Dąbrowska spent four years in Płonne (1925-1928), gathering material for her great epic novel, *Nights and Days*, is commemorated by a plaque.

The Chopin Centre in Szafarnia often organises concerts and other cultural events, including the prestigious International Piano Competition for Children and Young Pianists, held every May, as well as music workshops for children and master classes for university students. In the summer of 2009 the Centre introduced Chopin Picnics: visitors get a basket filled with local *specialities*, which they can enjoy in the park while listening to music.

The park in Szafarnia

The palace in Szafarnia

The palace interior; concerts of Chopin's music are often held here

A collection of Chopin head and bust sculptures in Szafarnia

A bust of Chopin by Wacław Szymanowski

Ugoszcz

Miss Tekla Borzewska danced with me twice, and I amused her with conversation, and as is customary, I was immediately heralded as her beaux and fiancee, until some chap or other finally cared to right the mistake; later they even came to know my given name, and the tailor, when I stood to dance with Mrs Dziewanowska in the leading pair, announced: now Mr Shopeh and Her Ladyship.

Excerpt from Fryderyk's letter from Szafarnia to his parents

During his holidays in Szafarnia young Fryderyk enthusiastically participated in all games and amusements, displaying outstanding dancing ability and agreeable manners; both of these talents were useful during the harvest festival. That was a time when everyone united in celebration, and even a farm hand, if he could muster the courage, could ask a lady to dance. Tekla Borzewska was a cousin of the Dziewanowskis' and visited them often. She was the daughter of Antoni Borzewski, owner of the Ugoszcz estate, who graciously repaid the hospitality of his Szafarnia relations, and Fryderyk was also frequently one of his guests.

The old Borzewski mansion is no longer there. The Ugoszcz park we can admire today, with its impressive tree specimens, some of which are 150 or even 200 years old, was set up only in the second half of the nineteenth century, and then rearranged at the beginning of the twentieth century. It is surrounded by a wall with an elaborately ornamented Neo-Rococo entrance gate. In the centre of the park, on the elevated bank of Lake Ugoszcz stands a two-storey, roughly rectangular palace in the eclectic style, with a colonnaded portico in the front, pentagonal orangerie on the eastern side, and a risalit, crowned with a two-storey tower, on the western side. It was built by Julia Borzewska, nee Piwnicka in the 1860s, when her family grew wealthy due to the success of their sugar factory in nearby Ostowit. Nowadays the building houses the "Kombatant" residential Social Welfare Home.

Situated in the community of Brzuze, in Rypin County, and with a population of around 600, the small village of Ugoszcz went down in history not only as a place visited by Chopin, but has another claim to relative fame: when in 1704 archbishop Konstanty Józef Zieliński, persecuted by king August II the Strong for crowning Stanislaus Leszczyński king of Poland, took refuge in Ugoszcz for a time.

The palace in Ugoszcz

Gulbiny

There were many guests at Szafarnia on Saturday: Mr Podowski, Mr Sumiński, Mr and Mrs Piwnicki, Chamberlain Piwnicki, Mrs Borzewska and her brother, Mr Dziewanowski, and Mr Wybraniecki with Mr Białobłocki. On Sunday we called on the Piwnickis in Gulbiny.

Excerpt from
Fryderyk's letter to parents

When Fryderyk visited Gulbiny, the owner of the estate was Alojzy Piwnicki; he was married to Brygida, the sister of Juliusz Dziewanowski of Szafarnia, so it seems the social life of the area was practically contained within the family of Fryderyk's friend Domuś. The old Gulbiny manor house was a traditionally built, but modest building, with a thatched roof and a spacious porch with elements of masonry. Around it stretched a beautiful terraced park, sloping gently down to the edge of Lake Dłuskie; the picturesque scenery must have made an impression on Fryderyk, as he repeatedly mentioned Gulbiny in his correspondence.

Over time, the manor fell into ruin, and it was demolished in 1959, but the softly rolling hills around it, overgrown with ancient trees, still charm visitors, and today they can also stroll along the new pier, recently built on the lake shore.

The unspoiled, diverse natural landscape, with its 15 lakes where storks, herons, cranes and cormorants hatch their young, is the biggest attraction of the commune of Brzuze, to which belong both Ugoszcz and Gulbiny, located about 12 km from Rypin. In the neighbouring villages of Żal, Somsiory, Kleszczyn and Mościska, archaeologists have unearthed remnants of medieval settlements, and in Studzianka, next to the Holy Family sanctuary in the old Pardon Chapel erected in 1704, a spring burbles, hailed for its miraculous properties.

Commemorative tablet in Obrowo

Obrowo

Harvest festivities were held in Obrowo today. The whole village gathered in front of the manor and everyone was having a splendid time, especially after they'd had a few vodkas; the village girls, in their half-out-of-tune voices, sang the old, familiar song: There's ducks in the yard, clucking in the mud, Our Mistress, she is all in gold and silver clad, There's a string, it is hanging from the tree in the yard, Our Master, he is out after playing cat and mouse, There's a snake, it is hanging from the branch in the tree, Our sweet Marianne, she is soon to marry, There's a bonnet in the mud, it was clean, now it's soiled Our maid, she's a dunce, tell me something I don't know.

Fryderyk Chopin to his family in the *Kuryer Szafarski*

That visit to Hieronim Romocki's house in Obrowo, and particularly the August harvest festival made an unforgettable impression on the fourteen-year-old Fryderyk. He drank in the folk music of Dobrzyń with all his soul, listening to village musicians, memorising the songs, admiring the dances and enthusiastically joining in himself; on one occasion he even took the bow from a player and played the double bass. Obrowo became a recurring theme in his letters, especially after Dominik Dziewanowski married the family's daughter, Józefa Romocka. More than a decade later, Fryderyk's sister spent a month there and, describing her stay to her brother, she concluded: everyone here remembers you fondly.

The Obrowo mansion was built in the Neoclassical style at the turn of the seventeenth century, then in 1898 it was remodelled slightly, and it has been preserved in that form to this day. It is now the seat of the local government and houses other services. A commemorative plaque was placed on the facade in 2004, inscribed: During the years 1824 and 1825 Fryderyk Chopin stayed in this house and gave recitals here. He also took part in the local harvest festival, known as "the walking-about." Nearby, a section of the old park with a precious stand of trees has been preserved. The village of Obrowo now lies in the county of Toruń, on national route 10. The region was once famous for a unique regional style of house, and the so-called "dobrzynki," peasant cottages preserved from the nineteenth century that still stand in the villages of Dobrzejewice, Łążyn and Osiek, alongside charming churches from the seventeenth and eighteenth centuries. Obrowo is surrounded by deep forests, which are a paradise for mushroom hunters, and make up part of the nature sanctuary of the Drwęca River Valley.

The palace in Obrowo

Michał Stachowicz, Harvest Festival, *1821*

Obory

In the summer of 1824 Fryderyk F. Chopin visited the Obory church and played this organ.

Inscription on the church wall
in the Carmelite Brothers monastery in Obory

The Carmelite monastery in Obory was one of the many places in the Szafarnia area that Fryderyk visited during the two summers he spent with the Dziewanowskis, who had been helping support the friars financially for generations. Fryderyk mentions Obory several times in various, and sometimes facetious, terms, as can be seen in a mischievous excerpt from the Kuryer Szafarski, dated August 16, 1824:

A local gentleman wished to peruse "The Monitor," so he sent his servant to the Carmelite Brothers, asking for "a periodical" to read. The servant, who had never heard the word before, asked the monks for a "hemorrhoidal" paper.

However, what was probably interested Fryderyk most was the church's nine-register, three-tower seventeenth-century Baroque organ, decorated with sculptures depicting King David with a harp in the company of angels playing a variety of instruments.

The original wooden church on Grodzisko Hill, known locally as the Calvary Church, was erected in the early seventeenth century for Calced Carmelite friars (not to be confused with the Discalced Carmelites, who observed a much stricter rule). Destroyed by fire just a few years later, it was replaced with another wooden church, and when that one became too cramped, the Carmelites began construction on a mortar church, finally completing it at the end of the eighteenth century. The crowning glory of the monastery is its imposing, forty-five-metre-high rectangular tower, which is an important local landmark. The Baroque-Rococo interior contains a number of valuable items of ecclesiastical architecture, including the main, side, and corner altars, the Providence Chapel, with its "Eye of the Lord," symbolising the omnipresence, eternal vigilance and paternal concern of God. Pilgrims, however, mostly travel to Obory to pray at the miraculous statue of Our Lady of Sorrows, also known as the *Obory Pieta*. The small, scarcely sixty-five-centimetre-high figure carved out of linden wood and covered with colourful polychromes – depicts the Madonna leaning over the body of the crucified Christ as he rests on her lap. The figure is shielded behind a protective cover, and every unveiling is accompanied by the sound of fanfare. Next to the church is the Carmelite monastery, built in 1741-1753 and nearby stands the seventeenth-century Holy Cross Chapel, remodelled two hundred years later. The church cemetery lies a short distance away.

The new addition to the complex is the 15-Station Way of the Cross, a symbol of the faith of the locals and pilgrims, built in 2004-2005 to celebrate

The village, situated in the community of Zbójno, in Golub-Dobrzyń County, is surrounded by a picturesque landscape, formed by low, rolling glacial hills, known as the *Drumliny Zbójeńskie*, separated by ponds, the trough of the River Ruziec, and the Działyńskie-Wielgie lakes. Because of this enchanting lake-and-hills scenery the region is referred to as "the Switzerland of Dobrzyń."

the 400th anniversary of the Sanctuary, and a year-round Nativity Scene. The monastery's tragic history is commemorated in the Martyrology of the Polish clergy, established in the church vault, in honour of the memory of priests who were imprisoned there by the Tsarist regime for supporting the January Insurrection (1863), and those who were brought and held in Obory by the Nazis, before being moved to German concentration camps, where the majority of them were murdered.

The Stations of the Cross near the church in Obory

The interior of the Obory church

The Obory church organ

Golub-Dobrzyń

On the 26th inst. His Lordship Pichon visited Golub.

Entry in the *Kuryer Szafarski*, August 1824

In the summer of 1824 His Lordship Pichon, aka Fryderyk Chopin, accompanied by Dominik Dziewanowski and his sister Ludwika, took a sightseeing trip to Golub.

Separated at the time from left-bank city of Dobrzyń by the River Drwęca, Golub was a separate town; what is more, the dividing waters constituted the border between two of Poland's partitioners, separating the Prussian town of Golub from Russian Dobrzyń.

When Chopin visited Golub, it had been on the map of Polish history for almost six centuries. The appearance and character of the town were first shaped by the Teutonic Knights, who recognised the strategic value of the high river bank and at the turn of the thirteenth century erected a fortified stronghold there. It was later captured by King Ladislaus Jagiello, who according to Jan Długosz's chronicle, *"dined in the castle, and then crossed the River Drwęca."* It was he who incorporated the castle and town into the Polish Crown.

One of the most highly regarded rulers in the history of Golub was Anna Vasa, the sister of King Sigismund III, who was the castle *starost* from 1611 to 1625. She was a well-educated, open-minded, modern woman, who not only remodelled the castle in then fashionable Renaissance style, but also managed to turn it into a vibrant centre of cultural and intellectual life whose fame extended beyond the borders of Poland. Unfortunately, in the years that followed, having suffered severe damages during the Swedish Deluge, Golub began to fall into decline. While still reasonably prosperous, mainly thanks to trade, by Chopin's time it had long lost its former glamour. The stronghold, which had some personal connotations for young Chopin – its last *starosts* had been the Counts Skarbek – also suffered during the partitions. The resident forest ranger, Richter, out of meanness had dismantled the timber gallery and used it for firewood, while the Prussian commissariat, which succeeded him, limited itself to carrying out most urgent repairs in the living quarters.

Given his attachment to the Skarbek family, the Golub castle must have been the main goal of Fryderyk's sightseeing tour; though he probably also visited the town itself, situated at the foot of the old stronghold, with its churches, historic houses and remnants of the fourteenth-century defensive wall. According to an article, published in 1899 in the magazine "Echa Płockie i Łomżyńskie" ("The Echos of Płock and Łomża"), signed by a "Józef of Drwęca", Fryderyk and his friends not only visited the town of Golub, but – if the text is to be believed – engaged in a mischievous prank.

A Lutheran church was being built at the time in Golub, and the party wanted to have a look at it. Upon finding themselves inside the unfinished temple, young Fryderyk and Dominik Dziewanowski stepped up into the pulpit. Then Fryc, speaking in Polish with harsh German pronunciation, began acting out a parody of a Protestant pastor, while Dominik, his arms inside Frycek's jacket, for greater comical effect, provided hilarious improvised gesticulation to emphasise his friend's sermon; this performance amused the present company so much, that, everyone, including the workers, fell over laughing (…) Then, as they were visiting the castle, an organ-grinder approached them, and Miss Ludwika gave him some money. Off the top of his head, Chopin made up an adequate rhyme to the grinder's music: For half a zloty, Miss Ludwika / wished for a Prussian waltz / If it weren't for her / we would never have heard / this Prussian music at all.

In 1951 Golub and Dobrzyń were joined into a single town, with a population of 13 thousand. Nevertheless, even after all these years, the old border is still visible: the historic old town and castle, the industrial park near the railway tracks, as well as the rural areas lie in Golub, while Dobrzyń is the residential part of town, which is home to sixty percent of the population, and is where most of the educational institutions and other services are located. The main tourist attraction is still the Golub castle, rebuilt after World War II in its former Renaissance form, in keeping with Anna Vasa's original idea. It houses a hotel, and a museum with archeological and ethnological exhibits from the Dobrzyń region, from original medieval knights' arms to the collection of replica cannons constructed for the film industry, and including a large cannon which "performed" in the movie version of Sienkiewicz's "The Deluge." Every year numerous public events are held in Golub, and the best known, now of practically intercontinental repute, is the Great International Knightly Tournament held in July. Other events include: the autumn "Hubertus" Fox Chase on horseback, combined with carriage driving competition and race, a falconry demonstration, the November Elocution Competition, the New Year's Eve Party with the Stars, and medieval knightly balls.

Apart from the castle, worth seeing are also the fourteenth-century Gothic church of St. Catherine, with its majestic tower and Baroque interior, a historic house dating from 1617 with a Mannerist gable, and a timber house from the second half of the eighteenth century.

Golub-Dobrzyń Castle

A cannon in front of Golub Castle

Castle interiors

The castle courtyard

Sokołowo

I promised to be at your home yesterday, but I was only able to reach Sokołowo today. (...) you wouldn't believe how sorry I am, how very sorry!... So much so, that I don't want to leave. Why ever did I struggle all the way here by buggy only to find no one in, but at least you will know that I was here. That I came to bid you and your papa a fond farewell.

Fryderyk Chopin to Jan Białobłocki

Fryderyk's friendship with Jaś Białobłocki, who was five years his senior, stretched back to the days when the Chopins ran a boarding house at their apartment in the Kazimierz Palace. Jaś lived there as a pupil of the Warsaw Lyceum, and stayed on when he went on to study law at Warsaw University. Their friendship was abruptly severed by Jan's progressing illness and ultimately, his premature death of tuberculosis. During summer holidays Fryderyk had often visited his friend's home in Sokołowo, which was the property of Jan's stepfather, Antoni Wybraniecki; he always enjoyed staying there, as evidenced by an exclamation in one of his letters: *Ah, I caught a scent of Sokołowo!*

Situated just 4 km from Golub-Dobrzyń, in the fifteenth and sixteenth centuries the village was the family grange of the Sokołowski family then became the property of the Działyńskis, and still later – according to records – Antoni Wybraniecki built his beautiful palace there. In the second half of the nineteenth century, the following owner of the estate, rather than finishing the project, ordered the palace demolished, preserving only the cellars and some sections of the walls, which he incorporated into his new Neoclassical mansion. After World War II the estate was transformed into a PGR, or state agricultural commune. The palace, never renovated, was on the brink of ruin before it was rescued in 1979 by the state-run Toruń Landmark Conservation Workshop, which converted it into a hunting lodge. The park surrounding the palace has suffered as well, but several tree specimens have been preserved, including five ancient oaks and a magnificent 250-year-old linden tree. After the dissolution of the PGRs the Sokołów palace was taken over by a state treasury company, which runs a pheasant and partridge breeding farm there, as well as a small hotel.

The palace in Sokołowo

Nieszawa

While passing through Nieszawa, His Lordship Pichon suddenly heard a Catalani, sitting on a fence and singing her heart out. The phenomenon attracted his attention, the more so that despite having passed the fence and heard the aria twice, he was still unable to make out the lyrics, which left his curiosity unsatisfied; finally, he pulled three grosz coins from his pocket and offering the money to the singer, asked her to repeat the song again. She kept fussing and frowning for the longest time, refusing to sing, but eventually, persuaded by the money, she began to sing the mazurka, of which, with kind permission from the superiors and the Censor, the Editor quotes here but one verse: Look-ye here, o'er the mountains, how the wolf is dancin', Oh, but he don't have a wife, So he's mighty howlin' (encore).

Entry in the *Kuryer Szafarski*, August 1824

It is not known for how long Fryderyk stayed in Nieszawa. The only evidence that he was there is the note quoted above, which is about folk music, a subject that captivated him. He calls the girl on the fence a "Catalani," thus humorously comparing her to the Italian opera singer, Angelica Catalani, whom Fryderyk had heard sing in Warsaw, and who had awarded him, the "child prodigy," with an engraved gold watch after she heard him play.

It is also questionable whether Chopin had any further knowledge about the village of Nieszawa. This small hamlet, situated on the edge of the Kuyavia region, on the left bank of the glacial valley of the Vistula, had played an important part in Polish history centuries earlier. The first mention of the place dates from 1230, when Conrad of Mazovia bequeathed Nieszawa to the Teutonic Knights, who then established their southernmost stronghold there. After the victorious battle of Grunwald, in which the Teutonic Knights were crushed by the united Polish-Lithuanian forces, King Ladislaus Jagiello recaptured Nieszawa, and the two sides signed a truce, later confirmed by the Peace of Toruń (Thorn). Jagiello demolished the Teutonic fortress, erasing any trace of it, and in its place built a new castle and town. The left-bank Nieszawa was to be a counterweight against the influence of the then Teutonic-German Toruń; it earned renown as the site of enactment of the Statutes of Nieszawa, a set of concessions and privileges granted in 1454 by King Casimir IV Jagiellon to the nobility in exchange for their support in the Thirteen Years' War and successfully competed with the birthplace of Copernicus in trade on the Vistula. However, after many years of conflict and pressure from the Toruń's merchants, Nieszawa was finally moved 30 km upriver in 1460 to its present site as a condition of Toruń's submission to the Polish Crown.

What else might Chopin have seen, apart from the village singer, as he rode through Nieszawa? He must certainly have visited the fifteenth-century late Gothic parish church with its Baroque interior, the seventeenth-century Franciscan monastery and the Holy Cross church, the Neoclassical town hall, built in 1821, the ferry crossing on the Vistula; although doubtless it must have looked different then than it does today. All these historic edifices and sites can still be visited in the present-day Nieszawa, as well as a small biographical museum devoted to the life and work of the accomplished architect, draftsman, and painter, Stanisław Noakowski, established in his Nieszawa home. Nieszawa is still a miniature town; its population is under two thousand, and it is the smallest community in the Kuyavia-Pomerania Voivodship.

Its most recent cultural attraction is the relatively new August event, *Nieszawa Encounters with Chopin.* The summer of 2009 marked its third edition, during which, apart from music recitals, a tableaux was presented, entitled *Chopin and the Catalani of Nieszawa.*

Toruń

I have seen, indeed, all the fortifications from all sides of the city, with all the details, I saw the famous machine for moving sand from one place to another (...) also, the churches of Gothic construction, founded by the Teutonic Knights, of which one was built in 1231. I saw the leaning tower, the famous town hall, both outside and inside, whose greatest peculiarity is that it has as many windows as there are days in the year, as many halls as months, as many rooms as weeks, and that its entire edifice is most sublime, in the Gothic taste. Still, all of this does not surpass the gingerbread, oh that gingerbread, a piece of which I've sent to Warsaw.

Fryderyk Chopin to Jan Matuszyński

This is how Chopin summed up his impressions of the excursion he took from Szafarnia to Copernicus' native city in 1825. Giving in to the rivalry of sightseers, he continued: *Did you see anything at all in Puławy? You only saw a small part of what my eyes beheld in its entirety. You saw, I suppose, in Sybil's Temple, the single brick taken from the house of Copernicus, from his birthplace? Well, I saw the whole house, the whole place, even if now somewhat defiled. Just imagine, Dear Jasiu, in that corner of the room where this famous astronomer was given the gift of life, stands the bed of some German, who undoubtedly having stuffed himself with potatoes, does nothing but break wind there, and those bricks, one of which was sent to Puławy with such great ceremony, are crawling with bedbugs. You see, my brother, this German shows no respect for the great man who lived here; he lets whole walls go to ruin, while Duchess Czartoryska would not permit even a single brick to be disgraced.*

The Market Square and Town Hall in Toruń

Copernicus' House

The house where Fryderyk stayed

Toruń gingerbread

Tablets commemorating Chopin and the Skarbek family

Fryderyk clearly made a thorough, methodical tour of right-bank Toruń, exploring the nooks and crannies of its medieval Old Town. The city is really part of the Chełmno region and lies on the border of Kuyavia and Pomerania, but officially it belongs to Pomeranian Voivodship. The trip also had a certain personal significance for Chopin. Toruń was the hometown of professor Samuel Bogumił Linde, the pre-eminent linguist, author of the authoritative Dictionary of the Polish Language, and a great friend of the Chopins. It was also in Toruń that Count Fryderyk Skarbek was born, considered by the Chopins to be Frycek's true godfather. During his sojourn in Toruń Fryderyk probably stayed at the Fengers' townhouse, a magnificent eighteenth-century edifice, which was the property of Countess Ludwika Skarbek's father. On the wall of the house two commemorative plaques have been placed; the first is inscribed: *In this house Fryderyk Chopin stayed in the year1825, and the other says: In this house lived Fryderyk Skarbek, 1792-1866, an eminent penitentiary, economist, historian, man of letters. On the centenary of his death – ZSP (Polish Students' Union) in Toruń.*

So, how does the contemporary Toruń's historic Old and New Town compare to the city seen through the eyes of the fifteen-year-old Fryderyk? Put simply, it has been greatly beautified; a jewel of Polish Gothic architecture, it has been meticulously renovated and remains under permanent conservatorial care and supervision; and, inevitably, it has grown: new boroughs have sprung up on both banks of the Vistula, and the once Prussian town, which used to count about twelve thousand inhabitants, is now a large city with a population exceeding two hundred thousand.

Turzno

Tomorrow morning we are going to Turzno, and we are not to be back until Wednesday.

Fryderyk Chopin from Szafarnia to his parents

During one of his long Szafarnia holidays Fryderyk also set off on an excursion to Turzno in the Chełmno region, an enterprise which involved crossing the Russian-Prussian border. Turzno, where he stayed with the family of Augustyn Bartłomiej Działowski, was a long established, Polish home with strong traditions, and a bastion of patriotism in the then Prussian-controlled area. The Działowskis had a wonderful, well-endowed library, an art collection and a grand piano just waiting for Chopin to play it. It is known that he visited Turzno on at least one other occasion, during his trip to Gdańsk in 1827.

The palace-and-park complex in Turzno was developed by Augustyn Działowski near the old manor of the previous owners of the estate, the Zboińskis. It was designed by a well-known Polish architect of Italian origin, Henryk Marconi, whose works included, among others, the Branicki palace, the Andrzej Zamoyski Palace, and the Hotel Europejski in Warsaw, and St. Anne's church in the suburb of Wilanów. The palace is built in the eclectic style, and is completed with a gazebo reminiscent of a small gothic castle on the park grounds. At the beginning of the twentieth century its owner added a side wing with a colonnaded portico, connected with the main building by a semicircular gallery with walkways modelled on Classical Roman architecture. During World War II the palace was taken over by the Wehrmacht, and its interiors were remodelled to suit military purposes. After the war it housed local public institutions. Today the palace is the property of an entrepreneur from Toruń and is undergoing a comprehensive renovation, which is projected to be completed in 2011, when it will reopen as a hotel with a restaurant and a conference centre.

A romantic English-style garden stretches through the 16-hectare space surrounding the palace, with ponds and old chestnut, linden, maple and plane trees, as well as numerous specimens of exotic trees and shrubs.

The palatial complex is entered through an imposing gate, whose twin pillars are decorated with figures of aurochs. On the bicentenary of Chopin's birth in 2010 a bronze bust of the composer, cast from an original mould of the marble sculpture carved by the nineteenth-century artist, Bolesław Syrewicz (the original can be seen at the National Philharmonic Hall in Warsaw, and replicas in Międzyzdroje and the Jardin du Tuileries in Paris), will be mounted on a stylised pedestal in the park.

A Turzno country landscape

The village of Turzno belongs to Toruń county, and has a population of under a thousand inhabitants. Besides the palace, other sights worth seeing include the Neoclassical chapel, founded by the Jeżewski family at the end of the eighteenth century and an iron cross with two parallel arms, which was believed to protect the villagers from the plague; there is also a later roadside shrine to St. Anthony and an inn, neither of which Fryderyk could have seen during his visit.

Kikół

So, today in Płock, tomorrow Rościszewo, the day after Kikół, then for a few days to Turzno, and a couple in Kozłów, then quickly off to Gdańsk, and back home again!

Fryderyk Chopin from Kowalewo to his parents in Warsaw, July 1827

During his short stay in Kikół Chopin was a guest of Karol Zboiński, son of Franciszek Ksawery Zboiński, a friend of composer's family, and godfather to Fryderyk's youngest sister, Emilia. Kikół, situated 9 km north-west of Lipno, was at the time a small town nestled among the picturesque lakes of the Dobrzyń Lake District. The earliest records of the town date back to the thirteenth century, when it was described as a fortified settlement, and the seat of the castellany. It received the status of a town in mid-eighteenth century, but lost it as a result of Tsarist repressions following the January Insurrection of 1863, and has since remained a village.

At the end of the eighteenth century, on a low hill overlooking Lake Kilkolskie, separated from Lake Sumińskie by a narrow inlet, a splendid Neoclassical palace was erected, rectangular in shape, and surrounded by a stylised park. The palace windows on both sides offer a breathtaking vista of the lakes. The pride of the estate was the Knightly Hall, decorated with polychromes from the turn of the eighteenth and nineteenth centuries. For many years, the palace was spared the ravages of war, but its luck ended with the outbreak of World War II, when it was severely damaged. Meticulously reconstructed in the 1960s, it served for a time as a recreational and educational centre, until it passed into private hands after the fall of communism.

The palace in Kikół

Chopin bust in Kikół

Lakes near Kikół

Silesia

Lower Silesia
Places visited by Chopin
LESZNO 5
36 KROTOSZYN
KROTOSZYN 15
NOWA SÓL 3
LEGNICA 3
BOLESŁAWIEC 94
ZGORZELEC A4
JELENIA GÓRA 5
POLAND
GOLIŃSK 35
NÁCHOD 8
CZECH REPUBLIC
NÁCHOD 14
HRADEC KRÁLOVÉ 11
14 ČESKÁ TŘEBOVÁ
11 MOHELNICE 11
OSTRÓW WLKP. 25
8 KĘPNO
94 BRZEG
46 OPOLE
41 PRUDNIK 40
Górka
RAWICZ
Zduny
Wąsosz
MILICZ
Żmigród
LUBIN
Ścinawa
Prusice
WOŁÓW
Oborniki Śl.
TRZEBNICA
Prochowice
BRZEG DOLNY
Odra
OLEŚNICA
Środa Śląska
WROCŁAW
Widawa
Kąty Wrocławskie
Siechnice
JELCZ-LASKOWICE
STRZEGOM
Żarów
Jaworzyna Śląska
OŁAWA
Sobótka
Ślęża
718
ŚWIEBODZICE
Szczawno-Zdrój
ŚWIDNICA
WAŁBRZYCH
STRZELIN
Wiązów
Jedlina-Zdrój
Pieszyce
DZIERŻONIÓW
Niemcza
Głuszyca
Piława Grn.
BIELAWA
Grodków
Broumov
NOWA RUDA
ZĄBKOWICE ŚL.
ZIĘBICE
Radków
Bardo
Nysa Kłodzka
P.N. GÓR STOŁOWYCH
KUDOWA ZDRÓJ
KŁODZKO
Złoty Stok
Paczków
Otmuchów
NYSA
Szczytna
Duszniki-Zdrój
Polanica-Zdrój
Lądek Zdrój
GŁUCHOŁAZY
BYSTRZYCA KŁODZKA
Stronie Śl.
JESENÍK
RYCHNOV N. KNĚŽ.
Śnieżnik
1425
Międzylesie
Vrbno pod Pradědem
Žamberk
Králíky
Praděd
1491
Hanušovice
Jablonné N. Orlicí

We did not want to leave Wrocław; meeting the kind gentlemen to whom I delivered the letters for Scholtz had made our stay in the city so much more agreeable.

Fryderyk Chopin from Dresden to his family

Fryderyk Chopin stayed in Wrocław several times, passing through the city on his way to other destinations. In 1826 he stopped there for the night while travelling from Warsaw to Duszniki, and then again on his return trip. He was there for a third time in 1829, having stopped in Wrocław on his way from Vienna to Dresden. He visited for the last time in November of 1830, as he was leaving Poland, never to return. From his letters we can see that, at first, Wrocław struck him as a foreign, alienating place, but with time he grew increasingly fond of the city.

In 1826, Fryderyk, along with his sister and mother, stayed at the Rautenkranz, an inn on Oławska Street that no longer exists today. As a favour to his professor, Józef Elsner, he delivered some letters to the professor's friends. One of the men, Joseph Schnabel, he found at the Wrocław Cathedral of St. John the Baptist, on Ostrów Tumski (the "Cathedral Island"), which is one of oldest parts of town and one of a number of natural islets on the River Oder. The other, organist Friedrich Berner, he found at St. Elizabeth's church on Św. Mikołaja Street. Both of these churches, having weathered the storms of history, still stand today and continue to dazzle with their architecture and ornamentation.

The cathedral, containing elements of a previous church founded by Boleslav the Brave in 1000 AD, must certainly have made an impression on Chopin. When he was there, damage caused by a 1759 fire was still being repaired. The cathedral would only receive its present Neo-Gothic appearance after being remodelled between 1873 and 1875; however, the Baroque interior of Fryderyk's times would have been even more striking than today's, with its exquisite gilded ornaments, elaborate polychromes, epitaphs for deceased bishops, and sculptures by some of the most talented craftsmen of the era.

Ostrów Tumski (Cathedral Island) in Wrocław – beautifully lit cathedral towers

St. Elizabeth's, then the parish church of Wrocław, contains a masterpiece of sculpture; there stands the canopied tomb of the von Rybisch family among numerous statues funded by wealthy nobles and epitaphs in memory of respected merchants. Founded by Heinrich von Rybisch before his death in 1544, it instantly became a source of considerable controversy, as canopies were reserved for Royal tombs. The city burghers are said to have smeared the tomb in wheel grease in protest of the shocking arrogance of von Rybisch, an unpopular city council member and tax collector. Today, St. Elizabeth's is a garrison church. In 1970s it was again damaged by fire and parts of the building were destroyed, but the von Rybisch tomb survived unscathed.

Fryderyk visited Wrocław for the last time with Tytus Woyciechowski on November 6, 1830. In a letter to his parents he wrote: *We arrived most comfortably and in good weather on Saturday at six o'clock in the evening. We settled into our lodgings at the "Golden Goose," then immediately set out for the theatre, where they were playing Der Alpenkönig und der Menschenfeind, which has not yet opened in Warsaw.*

The Junkrenstrasse, where the "Golden Goose" stood, is now called the *ulica Ofiar Oświęcimia* (Victims of Auschwitz Street), and can be found near the Rynek

The Tumski Bridge and cathedral towers

Wrocław Town Hall

Solny (Salt Market) and Świdnicka, the city's main street. During World War II the inn where Chopin had stayed was destroyed, but many other historic houses have survived, including the house of the notorious Heinrich von Rybisch at No. 1 Ofiar Oświęcimia Street. The City Theatre, the one that the two friends hurried to immediately after their arrival, was on Taschenstrasse (Piotra Skargi street), but no longer exists. Nine years after Chopin's visit to Wrocław, the City Theatre moved to a new Neoclassical building on Świdnicka Street, now the home of the Wrocław Opera.

Nineteenth-century Breslau (the German name for Wrocław) suffered its greatest shock when, after a month-long siege, on January 5th 1807, it was captured by Napoleon's armies. In the aftermath, General Vandamme ordered the city walls demolished, a decision which would ultimately prove beneficial to the city; in 1813, when Wrocław came back under Prussian control, it began developing even more rapidly than before. In 1830 the population of Wrocław was scarcely eighty thousand: significantly less than Warsaw's nearly one hundred and forty thousand.

The heavy Gothic walls, the foreign language, the parochial cultural life: all of this made it very difficult for Chopin to appreciate the charms of the native town of his teacher and mentor.

Fortunately, he became friends with Joseph Schnabel, who was a bandleader: *As it happened, we were at the local Guild, where Schnabel, the bandleader, requested my presence at a rehearsal before their evening concert. The band performs three days a week here. I found there the small, as usual, orchestra that had turned up for the rehearsal (…) Schnabel, who had not heard me play in four years, asked me to try out the piano. It would not have done to refuse, so I sat down and played a few variations.*

The present Teatr Lalek (Puppet Theatre) at 4 Teatralny Square was once the Guild Hall, but Chopin could not have played there, as it was not built until the late nineteenth century. The recital where Fryderyk both caused and evoked such a sensation was held at the older Grand Hall of the Merchants' Guild (also known as the Hall of the Hotel de Pologne) on Biskupia Street. The audience, while impressed with his technique, did not understand his innovative music: *apart from Schnabel, who was visibly overjoyed and kept grabbing me by the chin and patting me on the cheek; all the Germans were baffled.*

Though he still moaned: *it's so terribly German here; at least the company last evening was* – this time Breslau had shown a much more amiable face to Fryderyk.

It was really because of a chance acquaintance, a merchant by the name of Scharff, who, as Fryderyk wrote, *having hired a carriage, drove me around to see all the most stunning sights.* Where did they go? The author of the letter chose not to disclose. He left Wrocław on Wednesday, November 10, probably at around 2 p.m.

Duszniki

Having passed through Błonie, Sochaczew, Łowicz, Kutno, Kłodawa, Koło, Turek, Kalisz, Ostrów, Międzybórz, Oleśnica, Wrocław, Nimsch, Frankenstein, Warta and Glatz, we arrived in Reinertz, and here we still are.

Fryderyk Chopin to Wilhelm Kolberg

The very young Fryderyk Chopin, in a letter to a friend, gave a precise account of the places through which he had passed – not necessarily stopping in any of them – on his first great journey to take the waters in Silesia. While no evidence exists to prove that he had ever even stepped out of the carriage, even if only to stretch his legs, in **Oleśnica** (30 km before Wrocław), its citizens were so proud even to have been mentioned by Chopin that they chose to commemorate his "stay" by erecting a bust of the composer. It stands in front of a historic building which houses the State Music School named in his honour as well the Lower Silesia Music Society (between Kościelna and Matejki Streets).

The reason for the trip was clear – Fryderyk's and his sister Emilia's poor health. They were both to take the cure at Reinertz (today Duszniki Zdrój), heralded in 1825 as the best health spa in Germany, and where Józef Elsner had stayed the previous year. The younger children were cared for by their elder sister Ludwika and their mother. The family stayed at the Bürgel House, which offered food and lodging, on the site now occupied by the health spa "Nokturn" on Zielona Street; on the wall of the spa pavilion is a commemorative plaque.

Fryderyk was utterly bored by the daily rituals of the spa, which consisted of walking to the springs and ceremoniously drinking several cups of the healing water with added goat's-milk whey and herbs. He wrote to his friend:

By six o'clock in the morning at the latest, all the patients are at the spring. They only have the most horrid brass music here – a dozen or so caricatured numbers of varying tastes (...) and they put on plays for the shuffling convalescents; (...) This promenade to town along the lovely avenue joining Anstalt to the town usually lasts until eight o'clock, depending on the number of cups of water you're to drink in the morning (...) After dinner (...) the wretched music starts again, and so it goes until evening.

Duszniki – the Chopin Manor

Obelisk commemorating Chopin's stay in Duszniki

Day trips around in the surrounding area provided relief from the tedium: *there is a rocky mountain called Heuscheuer in vicinity of Reinertz, a place with breathtaking vistas, but because of the unhealthy air at its peak not everyone is allowed to go, and I am, alas, one of those patients to whom it is forbidden. But, no matter: I have already climbed a mountain called Einsiedelei, because a hermit lives there (...), and admired the splendid panorama of all Reinertz. We are to be going to Mount Hohemenze, which they say is a mountain in beautiful surroundings, and I think we will make it there...*

The rocky mountain, which Fryderyk was not permitted to climb, is known today as Szczeliniec Wielki, and *Hohemenze*, where he was expecting to go is now Mount Orlica. The hermit's cabin he mentions was to be found near the shrine of Holy Trinity, erected on Rozalia Hill (560 m.) after the plague of 1680. It is believed (based on Ludwika's anecdote) that Fryderyk visited an interesting factory on the edge of the town – a historic paper mill. In any case, it was on paper from that factory that he wrote his letters from Duszniki.

The most widely discussed event that summer was the sixteen-year-old Fryderyk's first public concert abroad, three years after Felix Mendelssohn, at the time fourteen, performed at the German spa. It was for a charitable, although somewhat unclear, cause. *Kurier Warszawski* (#22, August 1826), wrote: *(...) when several children were orphaned by the death of their father, who had gone to the springs to take the cure, Mr. Chopin, persuaded by persons aware of his talent, gave two concerts in support of the children, earning great admiration, and aid was rendered to the unfortunates.* An alternative, more romantic version of the events was quoted in August of 1892 by *Echo Muzyczne* (The Musical Echo): the orphan who Chopin's concert benefited was a lovely girl named Libusza, with whom the young Fryderyk was rather taken, and who served the spring water to patients. That version holds that her father, a labourer, died in the local iron foundry. In truth, no labourers or

The historic paper mill

patients passed away during Chopin's stay, but rather a master tailor named Joseph Schoor, who left behind four little ones. It has, however, been established beyond doubt that the concert (or concerts) did take place and at the hall in Spa Theatre, a building erected in 1810, and the centre of the cultural life of Duszniki. The greatest inconvenience the musical perfectionist Chopin had to suffer was the lack of a decent piano: *the one thing all the charms of Duszniki cannot replace.* Thus, on August 16, 1826, Chopin's international debut came about.

The old spa theatre, in the Spa Park, is now known as the Chopin Manor (Dworek Chopina). Since 1946 the town has held its own Chopin Festival, expanded in 1989 to include workshops for young pianists. Since 1963, the Manor has hosted the *Nocturnes* festival, a series of evening concerts held by candlelight.

The centrepiece of the old *kurhaus* in the Spa Park was once a plaster statue of Chopin's head, cast from the monument in the Royal Baths Park in Warsaw.

Chopin monument in Duszniki

The concert hall in the Chopin Manor

In 1995 it was replaced by a piece by Jerzy Teper, a sculpture made from the whitest Italian marble. Another Chopin likeness, created by Jan Kucz, was unveiled 150 years after the memorable concert, and set in front of the Manor, on the side of the building facing the Park. Opposite the Spa Theatre stands an obelisk with a medallion of Chopin, founded in 1897 by a Warsaw merchant, Wiktor Magnus. It bears an inscription, which translates: *With his true artistry and his cultured bearing, he revealed the noble character of his soul at the dawn of his youth.* The inscription is in Latin, because Mr. Magnus would not agree to an inscription in German, and the authorities of Reinertz refused to have it done in Polish.

Several sites in Duszniki have been named after Chopin, including a spring (Pieniawa Chopina), the avenue connecting the Spa with the town, two residential developments and a hotel.

All the sites in Duszniki associated with Chopin are marked by plaques. Most have changed little since his visit. Even the historic paper-mill has remained unchanged (although it may be in better repair now), where they not only sell hand-made paper pressed with rose or violet petals, but also allow customers to make it themselves.

Former Holy Trinity Chapel in Duszniki-Zdrój

Pomerania

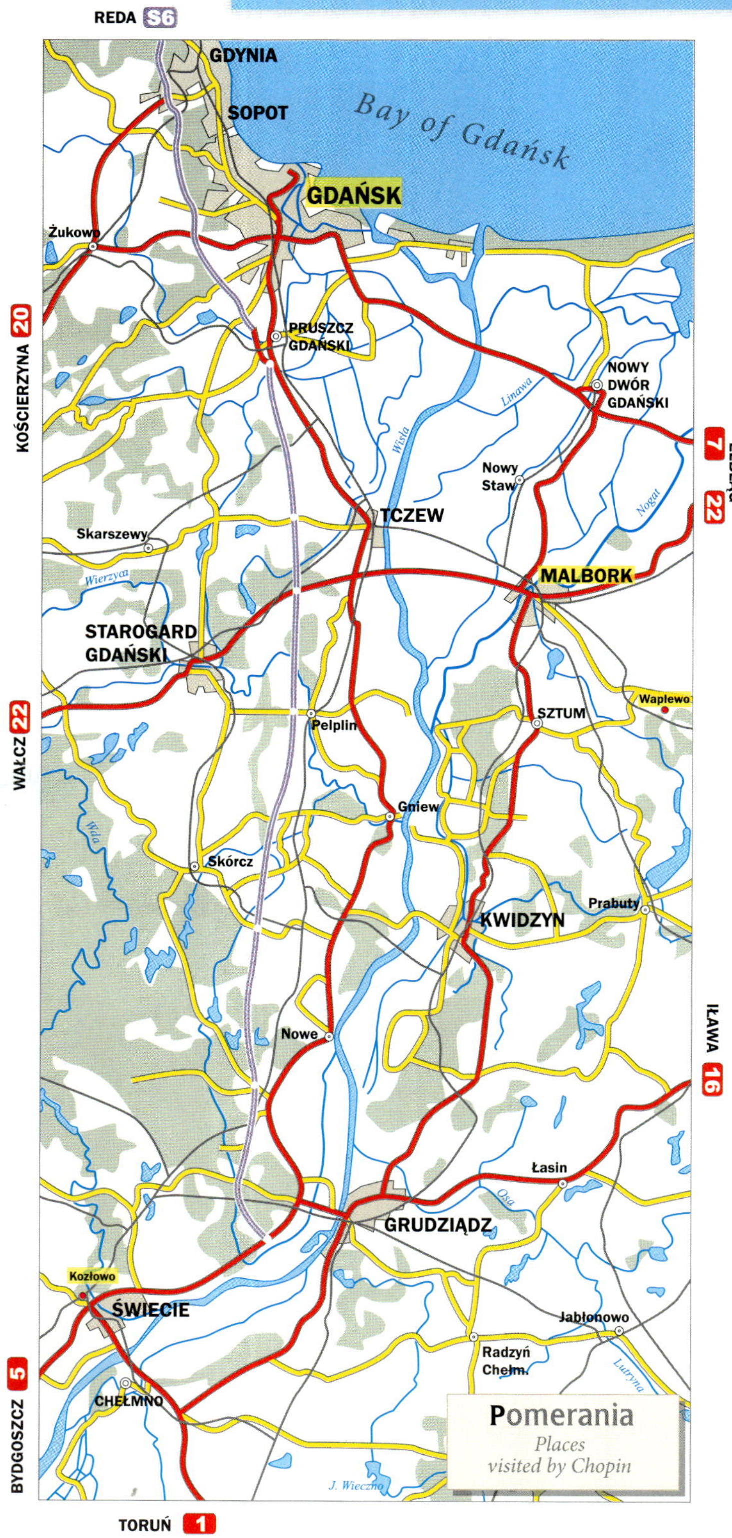

Pomerania
Places visited by Chopin

Gdańsk and Kozłowo

Since we're leaving for Płock, it would be madness on my part not to mention it. So, today in Płock, tomorrow Rościszewo, the day after in Kikół, then for a few days to Turzno, and a couple in Kozłów, then quickly off to Gdańsk, and back home again.

Fryderyk Chopin to his parents, 6 June, 1827

Fryderyk reminded his parents that he had been planning a journey to Pomerania – to Gdańsk and Kozłowo to be precise, in the company of several friends, one of whom, according to his biographers, was Count Ksawery Zboiński. However, none of the original sources confirm that the trip actually took place, or if it did, what places the seventeen-year-old Fryderyk visited. The trip would likely have taken place in July 1827. It was then that Fryderyk visited West Prussia's largest city, Gdańsk, known as Danzig at the time, stopping along the way at Ksawery Zboiński's family home in Kozłowo, now on the outskirts of the town of Świecie.

Researchers assert that if the travellers had chosen to stay overnight in Gdańsk, they would have probably stopped at the "3 Mohren" (The Three Moors) hotel, which was near the church of the Holy Trinity. It's also possible that they would have visited Jan Wilhelm Linde at his house at 1859 Tobiasza Street, which no longer exists today. Linde was the pastor at the Holy Ghost Church and brother of Samuel Linde, the vice-chancellor of the Warsaw Lyceum. During a walk in the Old Town of Gdańsk Fryderyk and his companions would have admired the Artus Court, St. Mary's Cathedral, the Neptune fountain and the Long Embankment with its fifteenth-century dock crane, reflected in the waters of the River Motława.

All of these historic buildings, badly damaged during the Second World, War have now been restored to appear just as they would

The Gdańsk Crane on the Long Embankment

have in Chopin's times, including the Basilica of the Ascension of the Virgin Mary, which burned to the ground, and the Gdańsk Crane, eighty percent of which was also destroyed by fire. The surroundings have changed, but the dark-red brick and timber Crane, the symbol of the port city, and now the seat of Gdańsk Maritime Museum, still extends out over the Long Embankment. No less impressive is the fourteenth-century Artus Court, redecorated in the seventeenth century with statues of the heroes of antiquity, and busts of King Sigismund III Vasa and his son, Prince Ladislaus at either side of the gate. In front of the Artus Court, just as in Chopin's times, the oldest secular statue

The famous Neptune fountain

The Long Market Street and Gdańsk Town Hall

in Poland, the enchanting Fountain of Neptune, continues to dazzle. Cast in 1615, this bronze Mannerist sculpture of the Roman God of the Sea received its spectacular Rococo fountain base in 1762. After a partial reconstruction, necessary due to war damage, it has been restored to its original charm.

Along with its farm outbuildings, mill, distillery and brewery, the Zboiński manor in Kozłowo, where the travellers stayed for a few days, was less fortunate. It was in West Prussia, on a site that is now a suburb of Świecie, in Kuyavian-Pomeranian Voivodship. In Chopin's times the master of the 300-hectare estate was "Mr. Zboiński," as Fryderyk called him in his letters; that is, Count Ksawery Zboiński, the very same gentleman who owned Kowalewo near Płock. No trace remains of the Kozłowo manor buildings today, but a commemorative stone reminds us of composer's stay, placed in 1985 by the regional branch of the PTTK (a state-run tourism office) in Świecie, and bearing the inscription: *In memory of Fryderyk Chopin's stay in Kozłowo and Świecie in the summer of 1825.* All the facts seem to be in order, except for the date; which may be correct after all, as Chopin may have very well have visited twice.

Waplewo

Antoni Sierakowski of Waplewo (...) was a lover of the arts, heart and soul; above all he was a musician, who played the violin very well, composed his own music and published it. The famous composer Chopin was his friend and guest at Waplewo.

Andrzej Bukowski, *Waplewo*

A significant stopping-off point on Chopin's journey through Pomerania may have been the Sierakowski estate in Waplewo, in Sztum County. Their host at the palace, which, among other attractions, offered a distant view of the Malbork Castle, was Antoni Sierakowski, a descendant of a well known Cracovian musician and writer Wacław Sierakowski. Among Waplewo's guests were such eminent personages as the writer Józef Ignacy Kraszewski, the painter Jan Matejko, and Oskar Kolberg, the eminent ethnographer, folklorist and composer. According to Andrzej Bukowski, author of the book *Waplewo*, Fryderyk stayed there from the 15th to the 20th of August 1827. While there are no original sources to verify them, the lines quoted above referring to Chopin's visit appeared in Antoni Sierakowski's biography, written in 1889 by his grandson, Adam Sierakowski.

The palace in Waplewo, 15 km east of Sztum, was built by the Sierakowski family in the first half of seventeenth century, surrounded by a formal park decorated with sculptures and gazebos. This oasis for ...ts remained unchanged when the young composer visited. Music ...ssion of his hosts, Antoni Sierakowski and his wife Antonina ...wska nee Zboińska; during those few August days that Chopin ...as their guest, the exquisite palace interiors, richly ornamented with sculptures and paintings, were filled with his music.

Over the centuries the property changed hands many times, but both the palace and the grounds, despite having been frequently remodelled during the nineteenth century, have been preserved. The Sierakowskis, whose coat of arms, the *Ogończyk*, is seen at the crown of the palace, were only able to return to Waplewo in 1999, fifty years after the property was parcelled out as a result of post-war agricultural policy. The present owner of the estate, Izabella Sierakowska-Tomaszewska, wife of the popular sports reporter Bohdan Tomaszewski, has established a Museum of Traditions of the Nobility at Waplewo, and its historic interiors, including the spectacular Gdańsk Hall, frequently resonate with Chopin's music. The most popular events are those honouring the composer's stay at Waplewo; they attract the most accomplished performers, and draw large audiences from all over Pomerania.

The park, created at the end of the eighteenth century, contains a Chinese pagoda, a statue of a nobleman, and natural landmarks in the form of ancient stands of beech, European ash, London plane and Eastern black walnut trees; they grew there during Fryderyk's youth, and are now over 200 years old.

The interior of the Waplewo palace

The palace staircase

Statue of a nobleman in Waplewo park

The palace in Waplewo

The Malbork Castle – the High Castle corridors

One of the chambers in the Middle Castle

Greater Poland

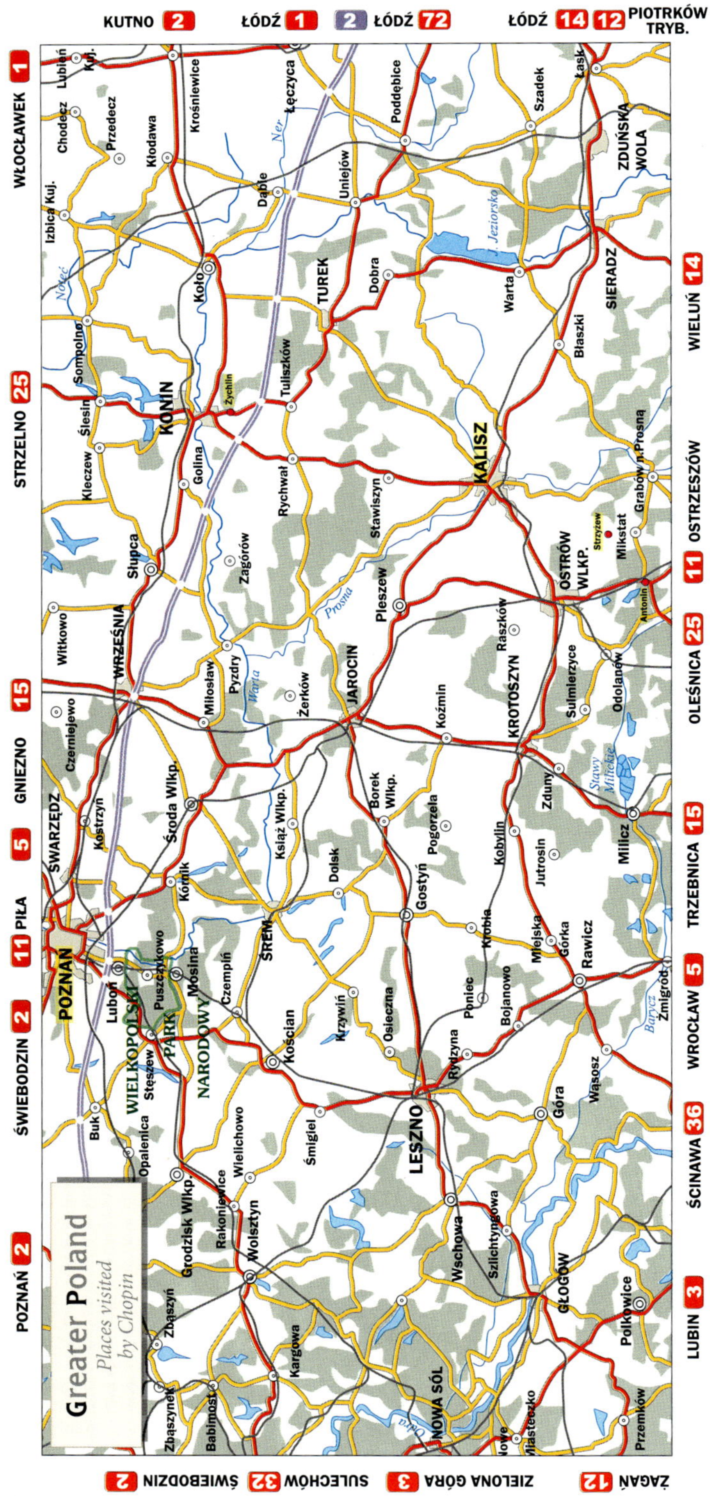

Kalisz

Coming back, I stopped in Kalisz and attended a soiree, where Mrs. Łączyńska and Miss Biernacka were present. The latter asked me to dance, and afterward I was obliged to dance a mazurka, with an even prettier, or at least equally beautiful young lady...

Fryderyk Chopin to Tytus Woyciechowski in Poturzyn

Researchers have documented at least six visits by Chopin to Kalisz – the first in 1826, on his way to Duszniki and back, and the last in November of 1830, as he was leaving Poland for the last time.

At the time, Kalisz was undergoing extensive reconstruction and expansion following the fire of 1792, which devoured practically the entire city. After the First Partition of Poland, the Prussian authorities ordered most of the city's old wall taken down (the 'Dorotka' bastion still stands). They also marked out a new main street, Luiza Avenue, now the Avenue of Freedom (Aleja Wolności); laid out the new city park, which with its abundant groves of ancient trees is now Kalisians' favourite place to meet and stroll; and built the first wooden Wojciech Bogusławski Theatre. After the fall of the Duchy of Warsaw, Kalisz found itself incorporated into the Russian Empire and attained new significance as an administrative, economic and cultural centre of Congress Poland. By 1825, impressive new buildings had appeared in the town, including the Voivodship School, the Tribunal Building, the Governor's Palace, the Stone Bridge, and the city toll houses, one of which, called the Wrocław Tollhouse, stylised to resemble an ancient building, is now a popular sweetshop, and one of the most identifiable landmarks of Kalisz.

Houses in Kalisz Market Square

It's unlikely that Chopin and his company could have overlooked those buildings, the more so that Kalisz was at the time a small town, occupying an area that was a fraction of its present-day acreage; in 1860 the population had not yet reached thirteen thousand.

The town on the River Prosna, which had developed so rapidly and prosperously over the nineteenth century, met a tragic fate at the very outset of the First World War. In August of 1914 Prussian forces literally annihilated the defenceless city with artillery fire, burning it to the ground. Ninety five per cent of the Old Town was reduced to rubble, and the population fell from sixty five thousand to a mere five thousand inhabitants. That we can admire the Old Town with all its magnificent buildings today, almost identical to those that Chopin saw, is a result of the diligent effort of the city government during the Second Polish Republic, and of careful conservatorial supervision during the rebuilding process. This was the first such reconstruction to be undertaken in the newly reborn Poland, and it was carried out in one of the nation's most ancient cities, if not the very oldest. The city of *Calisia* mentioned by Ptolemy in the second century A.D., may or may not refer to Kalisz – a matter of dispute among academics – but the ancient origins of the city are attested to nevertheless by traces of the ancient Amber Road connecting Rome to the Baltic, which have been discovered by archeologists near the city.

Today's charming, friendly city of Kalisz is the second largest municipality in Greater Poland, with a population of 110 thousand inhabitants, and its present – cultural, educational, and economic – is just as fascinating as its past.

St. Joseph's Church in Kalisz

Strzyżew

I am leaving at 7 o'clock tonight by coach to the Wiesiołowskis, near Poznań, which is why I'm writing in advance; I am not sure how long I shall be staying there, although I've taken a passport for a month. My idea is to be back in a fortnight. – The reason for this journey is also that Radziwiłł will be staying on his estate near Kalisz. He has made me all these propositions, that I should go to Berlin and live at his palace there, and tells me all kinds of niceties and pleasantries – I, however, fail to see how it would be to my advantage in any way, even if it were to come about, which I doubt it would, for as they say, a great man's favour is a fickle mistress, still, Papa is convinced that these declarations are not just des belles paroles on his part, and so I am going.

Fryderyk Chopin to Tytus Woyciechowski in Poturzyn,
October 1829

At the time, the Strzyżew estate was within the borders the Grand Duchy of Posen, in the Prussian Partition, and therefore "abroad" in relation to Congress Poland – which is why Fryderyk, already nineteen, mentions needing a passport. The estate belonged to Stefan Wiesiołowski and his wife Anna, *nee* Skarbek, who, as Fryderyk's godmother and his sincere protector, always sought to open up new opportunities for him. Strzyżew was adjacent to the extensive palace grounds of the Duke Antoni Radziwiłł, who was related to the ruling house of Prussia and a tremendously powerful potential patron for a young musician; the Wiesiołowskis' influential neighbour was not only a great lover of music, but himself a gifted (though self-taught) composer, cellist, guitarist and singer. Establishing contacts between Fryderyk and the Duke was a recurring theme during the young man's visits to his godmother's home.

No detailed description of the Strzyżew estate exists in any of the historical sources: only a somewhat cursory one by Fryderyk's sister Ludwika, sketched in her children's story entitled *Little Józio's journey from Warsaw to the Silesian waters*. The manor was surrounded by a cherry orchard, and next to it was a garden full of vebetables and strawberries and raspberries. The walls were hung with portraits of ancestors, and there was a clavichord in the drawing-room, on which the children of the house, a daughter and three sons, practised their lessons. In the 1840s Strzyżew was sold to the Prussian government, and the manor was pulled down, to be replaced in the 1870s with the eclectic building we see there today.

Nestled in the Ostrzeszow Hills, on the River Leniwa Barycz, 10 km from the county town of Ostrów, Strzyżew has a surprisingly long history. As early as 1295 it had already been listed as a royal village, and then for at least three centuries, from the beginning of the sixteenth until the end of the eighteenth, it was referred to as a city in various historical documents. Today Strzyżew is a large village with over a thousand inhabitants, and it contains several historic nineteenth-century buildings: a Neo-Gothic Polish-Catholic church and vicarage, the manor house, and its school buildings. The surrounding Ostrzeszów Hills are the highest in elevation in Greater Poland (Kobyla Mountain, 284 m) and are a Protected Landscape Park Area.

Antonin

I received your last letter, in which you sent me a kiss, at Antonin, at the Radziwiłłs'. I stayed there a week, and you wouldn't believe how pleasant it was. I had to force myself to leave, and returned by the very last post; and even then they would hardly let me go. As for me, and this temporary pleasant distraction, I would have stayed there until they turned me out, but my affairs, my Concerto to be precise, with its finale impatiently awaiting completion, beckoned me to leave this paradise behind. It was complete with two Eves: the young duchesses exceptionally kind and good, musical and tender creatures.

Fryderyk Chopin to Tytus Woyciechowski in Poturzyn, November 1829

Fryderyk Chopin's week-long sojourn at Antonin, the estate of Antoni Radziwiłł, the influential magnate and patron of the arts, as well as a gifted composer and instrumentalist, came after a legthy prelude. Prior to that visit, Fryderk had been to Antonin twice, the first time while he was staying at neighboring Strzyżew, and the second during his return journey from Berlin. The Duke, enchanted by the young genius, courteously invited Fryderyk's parents and sisters to visit Antonin; along with Count Fryderyk Skarbek, they arrived in

The palace in Antonin

August of 1829, and Chopin subsequently dedicated his new composition, his *Trio in G-minor, Op. 8 for the piano, violin and cello*, to the Duke with the intention of playing it together with his generous host, who in turn invited Fryderyk to visit him in Antonin again.

The palace in Antonin village, renamed in honour of the Duke from "Szperek," was built from 1822 to 1824, and designed by the famous Berlin architect Karl Friedrich Schinkel. It is a four-storey larch wood building, in the shape of a Greek cross, with an octagonal main body and with four, square three-storey wings added to the main sides. This spacious, sophisticated, and extremely comfortable residence was intended as a hunting lodge, and as the Duke was an enthusiastic hunter himself, he liked to invite his high-born guests to great hunts in the extensive forests of southern Greater Poland. In time, he chose to make Antonin his permanent, year-round residence, where he lived with his wife, the Duchess Fryderyka Dorota Ludwika

The interior of Antonin Palace

Hohenzollern, niece of King Frederic II the Great of Prussia, and their two daughters – Eliza and Wanda.

The Duke, who composed the first opera of Faust, based on Goethe's work of the same title – knew the most outstanding artists of the era, and turned Antonin a vibrant centre of culture, literature and the arts.

His two daughters were talented as well. The younger, Wanda, took piano lessons from Fryderyk: *All that time I was supposedly giving her lessons. She's a young thing, just 17 years old – and pretty, my Lord, it was enjoyable arranging her little fingers on the keys. But joking aside, she really does have a great deal of musical intuition, such that there is no need to remind her: now crescendo, now piano, faster here, slowly there, and so forth.* The other daughter, Eliza, during Chopin's stay painted two portraits of him, both of which he spoke of with great admiration. In the meantime he composed his *Polonaise in C-major*, Op. 3 for the piano and cello, intending to play it together with the Duke, and the host showed him his own still unfinished works.

The larch wood palace in Antonin was fortunate to survive both world wars unscathed and has been preserved in almost perfect condition to this day.

A sculpture of Chopin's head in Antonin park

In the 1970s it underwent a thorough conservation, and has been administered by Kalisz Centre for Culture and the Arts in recent years. The interior of the main body of the palace is made up of a three-storey Hearth Hall, also known as the Hunters' Hall, with a central pillar adorned with deer antlers and portraits of Duke Antoni, his daughters Wanda and Eliza, and Fryderyk Chopin; it is now a coffee shop and restaurant. A Music Salon has been created in one of the side wings; among the exhibits are portraits, a bust, as well as a post-mortem mask of Chopin and a mould of his hand. There is also a Buchholtz grand piano and an exhibit of publications about Antonin. The palace also has hotel rooms for tourists and attendees of the conferences, training sessions, and other events held there. At the main entrance there is a plaque with an inscription: *Fryderyk Chopin (1810-1849) was a guest at Antonin palace in the years 1827 and 1829*, and a bust of Chopin by Marian Owczarski stands in front of the building. The palace is surrounded

The Radziwiłł family at the table – drawing by Eliza Radziwiłłówna

An exhibit at the Radziwiłł palace

by a 12-hectare English-style park with a moat and numerous natural monuments, predominantly ancient oaks. The park also contains the chapel with the Radziwiłłs' tombs.

The surrounding landscape is enhanced by two fish ponds, Szperka and Wydymacz, which are now protected as a nature reserve.

Some of the annual events held in Antonin include the International Festival *Chopin in the Colours of Autumn* in September (held partly in Ostrów Wielkopolski), the International Exhibition of Musical Exlibris July and August summer concerts, and commemorative concerts on the dates of Chopin's birth and death.

With under five hundred residents, the village of Antonin in Ostrów County takes full advantage the popularity of the palace and of its lovely surroundings on the edge of the Barycza Valley Landscape Park, functioning as a summer retreat with swimming facilities and camping lodges on a reservoir; also worth visiting there are the forester's lodge and two Swiss cottages designed by Karl Friedrich Schinkel.

That evening Chopin performed several pieces by Haydn, Beethoven, and Hummel, either playing four-handed piano with Klingohr, the music teacher to the young and princesses, or with the distinguished host himself, who accompanied him on the cello. Chopin finished the evening with his own improvisations.

Ferdynand Hoesick, Chopin. Życie i twórczość *(Chopin. His Life and Work)*

Hoesick, quoted above, published a two-volume biography of Chopin at the beginning of the twentieth century, which for years was considered the ultimate authority on the composer's life and work. The event he describes was to have taken place in Poznań, at the Collegiate Square Palace, which was at the time

the residence of Duke Antoni Radziwiłł, appointed governor of the Grand Duchy of Posen by the Prussians. Some years earlier, in 1887, the same scene was immortalised by the eminent painter Henryk Siemiradzki in his work Chopin playing the piano in the salon of Duke Radziwiłł, in which we see Fryderyk surrounded by all the Radziwiłłs of Antonin. The painting became immensely popular in Poland, selling hundreds of reproductions, and could be found in many Polish homes as a patriotic symbol. The original can be seen at the Museum of Musical Instruments in Poznań, and was for decades thought to represent historical fact. However, contemporary researchers and experts on Chopin have expressed some justifiable doubts as to whether the concert took place at all. Chopinologists of the old school, like Hoesick, would sometimes use poetic licence in their works; for instance, no mention of Chopin's performance at the Governor's Palace in Poznań has ever been found in the original historical sources. What is more, it is questionable whether Duke Antoni was in Poznań at the time at all, leaving the historical accuracy of the concert ambiguous, as it is with many other incidents described in Chopin's biography.

Fryderyk Chopin giving a recital at Radziwiłł's palace in Poznań – print from the painting by Henryk Siemiradzki

The old Jesuit College

Still, there is no doubt that Chopin did visit Poznań. He spent several days there in the fall of 1828, at the end of September and beginning of October, stopping over on his return journey from Berlin. He had been invited by his parents' friend, Professor Feliks Paweł Jarocki, to accompany him to the German capital to attend a congress of "natural philosophers," as scientists were known in the terminology of the time.

The fountain in Poznań's Market Square with the Town Hall in the background

Regardless of any contemporary academic debate on the matter, a commemorative granite plaque at the entrance to the building that is now the seat of the Poznań city government proclaims: *Fryderyk Chopin played in this building in 1828.* The palace on Collegiate Square was originally built to accommodate a Jesuit college; and was later taken over by the Prussian government and used as the governor's residence. In the building's White Room, where the concert is to have taken place, stands a bust of Chopin designed by Marcin Rożek; its twin can be found in Poznań's Fryderyk Chopin Park.

Erected in the first half of the seventeenth century, the Poznań Jesuit College is a massive Baroque structure, which replaced the former Renaissance edifice; today it still combines the two functions it was originally designed to fulfil: that of a palace and that of a monastery – complete with the church of St. Stanisław on Gołębia Street, facing the Collegiate Square.

Another plaque commemorating the composer's time in Poznań has been placed on the wall of a building in Mielżyńskiego Street, near the Adam Mickiewicz monument; the inscription on it reads: To Chopin 1818-1849. The building houses the Poznań Friends of Science Society and the Poznań Academic Bookshop. Unveiled on the centenary of Chopin's birth, the plaque was destroyed during World War II, and then faithfully reproduced.

Also, a Chopin Room has been arranged on the first floor of the Museum of Musical Instruments in the Old Market Square. The most valuable exhibit there is the grand piano young Fryderyk played while staying at Duke Antoni Radziwiłł's palace in Antonin; there is also a post-mortem mask of Chopin, a mould of his hand, a bust of the composer sculpted by Wacław Szymanowski in lime wood, and finally, the painting by Henryk Siemiradzki mentioned earlier.

It has been documented that Chopin also visited Ostrów Tumski in Poznań (the cathedral island), where,along with professor Jarocki, he was a guest at the palace of the Archbishop of Gniezno and Poznań, Teofil Wolicki, who also happened to be a close relation of Fryderyk's patrons, the Count and Countess Skarbek. The history of the palace goes back to the fourteenth or fifteenth century, but it was to receive its present appearance in the nineteenth century. Ostrów Tumski, with the Arch-cathedral Basilica, St. Mary's Church, the Psaltery and the Lubrański Academy, which houses the exquisite collection of the Archdiocesan Museum, is the most ancient part of Poznań, and one the of the oldest and most precious historic complexes in Poland. Historians believe that it was there, in Ostrów Tumski, that the first ruler of Poland, Mieszko I, received baptism in the year 966.

The Poznań Cathedral

Żychlin

On the way back I attended the wedding of Miss Melasia Bronikowska; lovely child, she married Kurnatowski

Fryderyk Chopin to Tytus Woyciechowski, September 1829

The wedding Fryderyk described in that letter to Tytus was celebrated in the village of Żychlin, near Konin. Chopin attended it together with his travelling companions, Doctor Adam Bogumił Helbich, Alfons Brandt and Ignacy Maciejewski, on his return trip from Vienna. Doctor Heiblich thus reported the event on the pages of the Tygodnik Ilustrowany (the Illustrated Weekly):

Towards the evening we arrived at the palace. The host, in a joyful mood, greeted us with open arms, while numerous guests looked out at us of from all the windows. Soon we all felt at home, as if we were among our own loved ones (...) I shall not dwell on the description of the wedding celebrations. I will just say that time flew by like a shot, with the music, the dancing and general merrymaking. On the third day we were to leave. The young people were impatient to see their families in Warsaw. The horses had been harnessed and waiting since 11 o'clock in the morning, but has anyone ever left a hospitable home without being served breakfast first? So the horses had to wait. When noon came, the guests gathered in the hall. In the adjoining dining-room, to pass their time while waiting for the meal to be served, a merry company engaged in a lively conversation.

Suddenly someone proposed:

"To round off the amusements, let's play a game; and since we are all travellers here, let us play Traveller."

And so the names of the cities were distributed, and everyone made sure to be ready when called out; in spite of this, there was no shortage of forfeits.

When the turn for Mr. Henryk came to buy out a forfeit, one of the ladies asked him to do something that would equally please everyone in the company.

He took a moment to think, and ran outside.

He came back, bearing a branch of ivy, tied with a ribbon, and, having deposited it on Fryderyk's head, he pronounces:

"I hereby crown Talent and Virtue"

A long, thunderous applause sounded, and was reiterated over and over. Fryderyk had tears in his eyes, and they rolled down his cheeks, and they say there was not a dry eye among the company present.

Built on a rectangular plan with a front porch and pitched roof, the palace in Żychlin has been preserved to the present day and now houses a School of Economics and Services. A brozne plaque at the entrance states: *Fryderyk Chopin stayed here in the first days of September of 1829.* The palace is surrounded by a 2.5-hectare park with beautiful specimens of linden, plane and ash trees, considered natural monuments. There is also a Lutheran church maintained, in the Neoclassical style, also rectangular in plan, which was erected just a few

Portrait of Chopin –
drawing by Eliza Radziwiłłówna, 1829

The whole of the compact church complex is a typical example of the ecclesiastical architecture of Evangelical churches in Poland. The Żychlin church is the only Evangelical-Reformed parish in the country to have survived and continued its work uninterrupted since the times of the Reformation.

years prior to Chopin's visit, replacing a previous wooden building. The Neoclassical vicarage adjacent to the church was built some years later. On the site of the former church cemetery a Lapidarium has been established, displaying tombstones of historical and artistic value transferred to Żychlin from other disintegrating Evangelical cemeteries. The tombstone of the Bronikowski family here, in the shape of a miniature church is worthy of attention. After the bodies of the deceased were desecrated by the Nazis during World War II, the tomb was converted into a Mausoleum in which mementoes from the history of the Żychlin congregation are preserved.

Lesser Poland

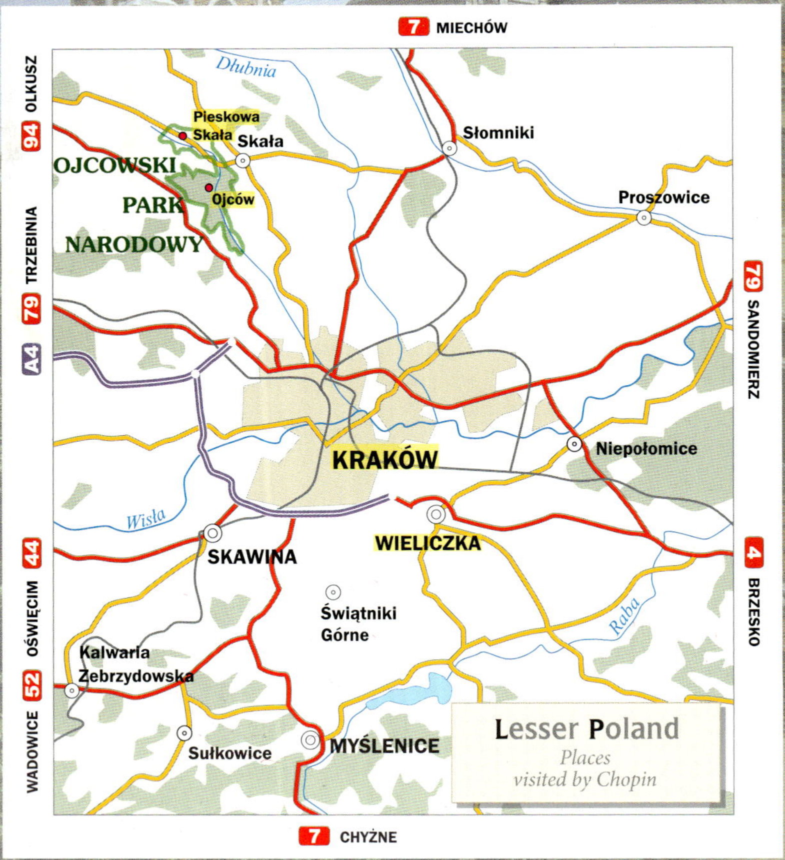

Kraków

The first week we passed sightseeing in Cracow and touring the surrounding area. (...) Cracow captivated my attention so much that I hardly had a moment to think of home, and you (...)

Fryderyk Chopin to Tytus Woyciechowski in Poturzyn

Fryderyk wrote this letter already from Warsaw, after he had returned from his both artistically and socially very satisfying summer travels.

He passed his final exams at the High School of Music on July 20, 1829, and having equipped himself with the necessary funds, he set off for Vienna. This time he travelled in the company of his peers. The oldest of the group, and therefore responsible for the whole expedition, was Romuald Hube, a lecturer at the Law Department at Warsaw University, himself only twenty five years old.

The first stop on their journey was Cracow, and Hube, having been a pupil at Cracow's St. Anne's Gymnasium for several years, was the best guide they could have wished for. It is not known where the young men found lodgings, as Fryderyk, preoccupied with the charms of the city, did not write from Cracow to anyone, even his parents. The travellers could have stayed at the House of the White Eagle (pod Białym Orłem) at No. 42 Floriańska Street, at an inn known as "Staniszewski auberge," founded in 1827. When they were hungry, they may have dined at the restaurant at No. 24, the building known as "Szynkarski House." Cracow's famed *Cukiernia Lwowska*, (the Lvov Confectioner's; now *Jama Michalika*) did not exist at the time – Jan Michalik would not open his famous *pâtisserie* at No. 45 Floriańska Street until 1895. In the house at No. 41 – today the Matejko House museum – already lived the parents of the best known Polish nineteenth-century painter, but Master Jan Matejko was not born until nine years later. His future teacher,

Cracow – Wawel Hill and the banks of the Vistula

St. Florian's Gate in a period engraving

Wojciech Korneli Stattler, was already living and working on that same street at No. 34, the Goślinowski Townhouse.

The medieval defensive walls surrounding the city centre had already been pulled down (1810-1814) by the time of Chopin and his friends' visit. Only a part of the northern section was preserved, along with a few of the original fortifications: the fifteenth-century Barbican, also commonly known as the "Rondel," or Saucepan; St. Florian's Gate, dating from the turn of the thirteenth century; the City Arsenal, then one-storey high; and the three bastions, the ones called the Haberdashers', the Joiners', and the Carpenters'. Those portions of the city defences were rescued by a Jagiellonian University professor, Feliks Radwański who, when purely historical arguments in favour of preserving them failed to

Cracow Market Square in an early nineteenth-century print

persuade the city authorities, resorted to…medical reasoning. Destruction of this last protective wall, he warned, will expose the city to harsh north winds, bringing *"terrible snowstorms,"* going on grimly to say that, *"women and children will be frequently afflicted with gumboil, rheumatism, and even paralysis."*

The weedy and boggy terrain exposed after the walls had been taken down had to be thoroughly drained and then replanted. This landscaping project lasted until 1830, and when Chopin and his friends were revelling in Cracow, the *Planty* Gardens, freshly planted with poplar and chestnut saplings and newly sown flowerbeds, were not the ideal location for leisurely strolls that they are today. Still, the young travellers must have admired the powerful fortifications, and looked for the Jagiellon Eagle on St. Florian's Gate' wall (the present Piast Eagle was sculpted by Z. Langman in 1882). Could the young Fryderyk, before setting out in "conquest" of the capital of the Austro-Hungarian Empire, have knelt down to pray before that altar, just as King John III Sobieski did before he charged the Turks encircling Vienna in 1683? At the time the altar was still in the Barbican, and was only moved to St. Florian's Gate in 1834. The shabby-looking bastions did not then have the galleries for guards we see there today, as they were reconstructed after the World War II.

Once the seat of the Polish royalty, Cracow was becoming a marginalised city on the outskirts of the great empire. Not only was the city wall demolished: many public buildings, including medieval churches, met the same fate. Of the old Town Hall torn down in 1817 due to its deplorable condition only the solitary clock tower has been preserved. Next to it, occupying the centre of the Market Square, stands the old Cloth Hall, which in Chopin's time was the venue for all kinds of ceremonies and celebrations; in 1809 a ball in honour of Prince Józef Poniatowski was held there. The Cloth Hall has stood since the sixteenth century, when two parallel rows of vendor stands, separated by a roofed aisle, were enclosed into one large structure with colonnaded loggias and attics crowned with turrets and sculpted faces.

The guests from Warsaw must have visited the Wawel Hill, despite the fact that the castle – the former seat of Polish Kings – had been burned and looted by the Swedes, deserted since the times of Sigismund III Vasa, stripped of the

The Cloth Hall and St. Mary's Church

The Wawel Castle courtyard

crown insignia by the Prussians, and was in the midst of the darkest days in its history. Nevertheless, in spite of those facts, or even in defiance of them, Poles cherished Wawel as the cradle of their national spirit and took comfort in its memories of glory, such as they were. Wawel Castle itself was turned by the ruling Austrians into a military hospital. They also removed all the medieval inner bailey buildings to make room for a parade ground. In 1815 Cracow's status changed to that of a Free City, and Wawel Hill was tidied up somewhat; some of the most important buildings were renovated, while the rest were demolished and cleared away. For Chopin, the cathedral had another important merit: it was the centre of Polish liturgical music, and he might have heard master organist Wincenty Gorączkiewicz play there.

The Wawel Cathedral was then and is today the most important Polish national religious site. It stands on the ruins of two previous Romanesque churches, from which only the crypt of St. Leonard survived the fire of 1305. Ladislaus I the Elbow High was crowned there within the walls of the still burned-out church in 1320. The enthronement of all subsequent Polish rulers (except Stanislaus Leszczyński and Stanislaus Augustus Poniatowski) took place in the new basilica, resplendent with its three imposing towers: the Sigismund Tower, famed for its bell; the Clock Tower; and the Vicar's Tower. The cathedrals' most valuable relic is the silver casket resting on the shoulders of angels and containing the remains of Bishop St. Stanislaus and St. Florian. In the nineteenth century, at a time when there was no true Polish state on the map of Europe, this Altar of the Motherland, before which the Kings of Poland had laid the trophies of their victories, had a particularly special meaning. The young company from Warsaw would surely have bowed their heads here.

We know for certain that Fryderyk visited the Collegium Maius, formerly the home of the Jagiellonian University Library. We can see the tangible proof of the composer's presence there, in the guest book, dated 23 July, 1829: his personal signature. That priceless autograph is preserved at the Manuscript Department of the Jagiellonian Library, at 22 Mickiewicza Avenue, the library's current location. The unique character of Collegium Maius was changed in the 1860s when it was remodelled in the Neo-Gothic style. After the Second World

War the *alma mater* of Poland was restored to its original form and the historic buildings now look just as they did during Chopin's sojourn in Cracow. The name of the educational institution is also the same: the Cracow Academy, founded in 1364 by King Casimir III the Great, had already changed its name to Jagiellonian University eleven years prior to Fryderyk's visit, in 1818. The history of Collegium Maius goes back to King Ladislaus Jagiello who renovated the edifice with the funds from the late Queen Hedwig's inheritance. The spacious building was built of cut stone near St. Anne's church and, on July 26, 1400, the first lectures were held there. After a fire in 1494 it was rebuilt as an imposing edifice with an inner courtyard.

The Jagiellonian University has grown over the years, but Collegium Maius has remained the jewel of the institution. It houses the Jagiellonian University Museum, with such exhibits as medieval lecture halls, musical instruments, scientific equipment (which is kept in the alchemy room), globes, and paintings by

The Wawel Cathedral

Polish (Matejko) and European (Delacroix) artists. The university treasury features the Gothic rector's sceptres, and gifts such as rings, gold chains, and a golden globe. Collegium Maius also fulfils a role as a showpiece for the University and the city, and is used as a venue for various events. The Collegium Assembly Room is decorated with portraits of the university's benefactors, predominantly Kings. In the Green Room stands the Pleyel grand piano which Chopin played during his stay in Scotland. There is no doubt as to the authenticity of the instrument

– inside the resonance box Chopin left his dated autograph: *Frederic Chopin, 15 novembre 1848.* The instrument belonged to Chopin's student and admirer, Jane W. Sterling, who assembled a collection of the Master's mementoes. The piano came to Cracow from Lyon, from the collection of the music critic Eduard Ganche.

Pigeons flying over Cracow Market Square, Adam Mickiewicz monument and St. Mary's Church

Sightseeing trips around Cracow

If nothing else, the sheer beauty of Ojców was worth getting wet for...

Fryderyk Chopin to family,
already from Vienna

In the description of Chopin's expedition to the Prądnik River Valley, the figure of Klementyna Hoffmanowa, nee Tańska appears quite often. She was editor-in-chief of *Dziennik dla dzieci* (Children's journal) and author of *Rozrywki dla dzieci* (Amusements for children), magazines which must have been among the favourites of the Chopin children. Her story of a trip to Ojców seems to have inspired Fryderyk and his company to follow in her footsteps when they found themselves nearby. Though hardly children, they insisted on spending a night at the home of a certain peasant by the name of Indyk, meaning "Turkey." *Izabella! ...it's exactly where Miss Tańska stayed! Fryderyk gushed in a letter to his younger sister. As luck would have it, though Mr. Indyk lives a mile away from Ojców, our driver, not knowing the way, headed in the direction of Prądnik.*

He was unable to turn the carriage around in a narrow canyon, so the travellers had to continue on foot, intrepidly wading across a river to get to their destination. Fryderyk was cold, so he bought a warm, Cracovian-style hat from Mrs Indyk. He cut it in two, took off his wet shoes, and wrapped his feet in the halves of the cap as improvised woollen socks. Finally protected from the cold, he was able to drink some wine by the fire and share a laugh with his "trusted mates," happy to be as if in the scenery of a ballet by Kurpiński's; whose *Wesele w Ojcowie* (Wedding in Ojców) had just been produced with resounding success in Warsaw.

No description exists of the following day of the trip, but it has been established that Fryderyk visited the Castle Mountain, and the Black and Royal caves; where "King Ladislaus I the Elbow-high concealed himself from his enemies" at the end of the thirteenth century. Certainly one of the reasons Chopin wished to see it was that *King Ladislaus the Elbow-high*, an opera by his beloved mentor, Józef Elsner, was playing in Warsaw.

The castle in Pieskowa Rock – period engraving

We can learn a good deal about what the landscapes of Prądnik Valley looked like at the time from the account of the talented Miss Tańska. The Ojców Castle was already in ruins, but the hill it stood on served as an excellent viewing point. *Only having stood at the foot of the tower, on a heap of rubble* – wrote Tańska – *was I able to observe the beauty of Ojców, for it is to be found not in the castle, but in the valley below, seen from its ruins. (…) On both sides of the valley stand rocks shaped like the strangest of houses (…), and it is impossible even to see to the end of this city of the Titans, and peaks of the rocks, overgrown with tall firs, reach up to the sky. (…) I could never grow tired of that vista.* The author also recorded the legend of the castle, built by Casimir III the Great, *mindful of his father's wandering over the caves and caverns. At first he called it 'Ojciec u skały' (Father's at the rock), and then just Ojców (Father's).* Fryderyk, an avid reader of Tańska's writings, saw these landscapes through her eyes. The Casimir castle, where decades earlier (1787) the last King of Poland had stayed, after the fall of Napoleon, uninhabited and abandoned, fell into decay. In 1826 one of its walls collapsed. When Fryderyk was in Ojców, the Austrian administration sold the derelict buildings to Konstanty Wolicki, who decided to tear it down almost entirely, leaving only the entrance gate and the tower. Soon after not even the "heap of rubble," mentioned by Tańska, was left of the fortress, but Fryderyk could still have seen it.

Today a model of the castle and an exhibition devoted to its history can be viewed in the gate building. Elements that still stand include an octagonal

Pieskowa Rock – the castle and the Club of Hercules – contemporary view

Dancing at a Cracow tavern
– *painting by Michał Stachowicz*

(though shortened) tower, sections of the living quarters and defensive wall, and a well that was once very deep, now only twenty metres, secured with a metal grill. Thinning out the trees there has uncovered the view of the ruins, making them picturesque part of the Eagles' Nests Trail (Szlak Orlich Gniazd). Seven kilometres further along stands Pieskowa Rock Castle. Fryderyk and his friends reached there too, as did the indomitable Miss Tańska.

The view dazzled her even from a distance: *suddenly, and quite unexpectedly, did I see before me all of Pieskowa Rock, and I simply forgot about the rest of the world. There was a range of new, higher, and still stranger rocks, the mountain itself, tall and broad, and on top of it a magnificent castle; on the other side a beech wood of freshest green, and the River Prądnik down the middle, (...) and then, nearest to my eyes, the famed Club of Hercules.* A closer look did not diminish her initial awe, for Pieskowa Rock was one of the best preserved of the castles built by Casimir III the Great. Numerous clues indicate that it must have been once a splendid fortress: *it is furnished with all possible amenities, a mill, a smithy, huge storage chambers...*

The fortress was at the time the property of the Wielopolski family, but throughout its history only one of the masters of Pieskowa Rock, Hieronim Wielopolski, lived there permanently, in the eighteenth century. An avid hunter and a talented craftsman, he set up a smithy and a woodworker's workshop there (making furniture was his hobby). He also walled up the Italian galleries and the loggia; he spent the winters there as well, and the Italian-style castle was hardly the warmest of abodes in cold weather. When Hieronim died, his family, clearly relieved, moved to Warsaw, and only spent the summers at Pieskowa Skała. It deteriorated under the ownership of subsequent owners. The castle had to wait until the beginning of the twentieth century before it was renovated, and then it was turned into an elegant pension, which remained in operation until the Second Word War.

After the war the castle was renovated again (the galleries and the loggia were restored) and after it was finished, it was converted into a museum. Today it is a regional branch of the State Arts Collection in Wawel. The awe-inspiring four-winged castle, with a clock tower and a terrace overlooking the landscape park, is a truly magnificent relic of history. The interiors are decorated with period furniture, sculptures, paintings and artistic crafts (from the fifteenth to nineteenth centuries). The view from Pieskowa Rock that young Chopin admired is still the same: the sixteenth-century fishponds along the Prądnik River, the Club of Hercules, and Wernyhora Rock.

One cannot lodge at Mr. Indyk's any more, but there are numerous other places offering accommodation. In the "Pod Łokietkiem" house is W. Szafer's Museum of history and nature; "Pod Kazimierzem" houses an education and information centre dedicated to the Ojców National Park, the smallest in Poland, measuring 21 square metres, and established in 1956. The southern part of the park is closed to motor traffic, but it is accessible on foot, by bike, on horseback, and by traditional horse-drawn carriages. Of the four hundred caves in the area, two are open to visitors – the same ones that Chopin visited: the Łokietka (Royal) Cave (320 metres long), and the Dark Cave (209 metres long).

The Prądnik River Valley

Wieliczka

The youths from Warsaw: Fryderyk Chopin, Alfons Brandt and Mieczysław Potocki set out on another expedition under the leadership of Romuald Hube – to Wieliczka, where they visited the famous Salt Mine. No records exist of Fryderyk's impressions of the place – but again, there is proof that he was indeed there, in the form of his signature, dated July 23, 1829.

Part of the mine was made available to the public as early as the eighteenth century, when the word of healing properties of its saline waters spread. In the nineteenth century, the reputation of Wieliczka reached high society – and venturing down to the salty underground became fashionable. Thanks to the tireless authoress Klementyna Tańska-Hoffmanowa we know that in those times descending into the depths of the mine was only for the bravest travellers. First one had to obtain a permit and have a guide allocated by the mine director's office. Then the adventurer had to put on a long, cloth gown: *in which they clothe the visitors for the protection of their garments,* and which, in Tańska's opinion, *seem to resemble the funeral garments of the dead.* The tourist-patient had two ways of reaching the mine: either descend the stairs, or slide down the rope. We do not know which way Chopin's company chose, but Miss Tańska and her friends had

St. Kinga's Chapel in the Wieliczka Salt Mine

boldly pointed to the rope. Afterwards she wrote: *We approached the entrance to the mine, which looked like a shed; inside it is a hole which resembles a giant well, and it is through there that both the workers, and the curious descend; peeking into the dark abyss into which one is to plumb sends shiver down the spine; the pen, with which one is to write down one's name in the special book of records, shakes slightly in the hand…*

Like all the other attractions Chopin visited in and around Cracow, Wieliczka today is a must-see for all visitors and since its inclusion in 1978 on the UNESCO List of World Heritage it has become a tremendously popular destination. Its unusual historical merits (the magnificent St. Kinga's Chapel, old mining machinery) and natural wonders (caverns with underground salt lakes) are worth going to great lengths to see. Today, however, no real effort is required – it is enough to buy a ticket and take the lift down to 135 metres below the ground level, where visitors get off and start their guided underground hike through the comfortable and safe corridors, while breathing in the healing, naturally iodised air. As the oldest salt works in Europe, the Salt Mine's Museum is able to exhibit some of the most priceless monuments of the salt mining industry and the most exquisite of salt crystals and sculptures, as well as the panorama of the old Wieliczka, and reproductions of the most valuable and historic signatures from the guest book, including that of Fryderyk Chopin.

A salt statue of St. Kinga, the patron saint of miners

The Chełm Area

I must tell you from the bottom of my heart, I have such pleasant memories of it all, and those fields of yours have filled me with some kind of nostalgia – that birch outside the window, I seem unable to erase it from my memory…

Fryderyk Chopin to Tytus Woyciechowski in Poturzyn

Dearest Tyciu or *Dearest life of mine* – letters beginning with those salutations often arrived at Poturzyn, because Chopin tended to solicit his friend's advice both on matters of the heart, and music (*when I'm working on something new, I would like to know what you think of it*). Tytus, musical by nature and having a reliable and stable character, was the son of a landowner from the Lublin region. The boys became friends between 1821 and 1823 when Tytus, then a pupil at the Warsaw Lyceum, lived at the boarding house run by Chopin's parents. After Woyciechowski graduated from the university the two friends had to rely on the post, to maintain their intellectual and emotional dialogue. Two years Fryderyk's senior, Woyciechowski returned to Poturzyn and busied himself with improving his estate; he was the founder the first sugar factory in the region. He rarely visited Warsaw, for which Chopin mocked him: *now I'm finishing a mill, now I'm building a distillery, now it's wool, now lambs, now the spring crop is finally coming up.*

Poturzyn, a village in the County of Tomaszów Mazowiecki, is far from Warsaw. Just one visit by Chopin to his friend's home has been documented – it was during the last summer he spent in Poland. He could never have left the country without saying goodbye, and besides, he wanted to persuade Tytus to go abroad with him. So, on July 9, 1830 Fryderyk set off on his long journey to Poturzyn. He passed through Piaseczno, Czersk, Ryczywół, and Kozienice, then crossed the Vistula and headed for Puławy, Końskowola, and Krasnystaw. There he switched to a "post-chaise" and having passed through Zamość, Komarów, Tyszowce and Oszczów, on July 11 he arrived in Poturzyn. He brought with him a printed copy of his Variations in B flat major which had just arrived from Vienna; he dedicated them to Tytus. The large manor house was covered with a pitched roof. On one side of the two-storey main body of the building there was a greenhouse, and on the other a one-story wing. The guest rooms were located upstairs, in the central part of the house.

The idyllic time he had spent in Poturzyn deeply affected Chopin. He wrote in one of his later letters: *(…) When I'm down and out, and have nothing to eat, you must hire me as scribe in Poturzyn; I shall live next to the barn, and I shall be as happy as I was that year at your manor house.*

The two friends had ten days for each other, which they spent swimming in the pond, shooting the crossbow and taking hiking trips in the area. And, in the nearby village called Stara Wieś, in the manor house of Count Poletyłło, there was an instrument worthy of Chopin's genius – a brown Pleyel. Fryderyk and Tytus played Chopin's yet unfinished *Piano Concerto No.1* in E-minor in four hands, to the utter delight of the host's daughter, who would later become Tytus' wife. Iwaszkiewicz suggests that Poturzyn landscapes and the nostalgic songs, called "dumki," sung by young village girls working in the fields inspired Chopin's *Nocturne in G-minor*, in which subtle, melancholy Ukrainian notes shine through. Today we are reminded of Chopin's first and only stay to Poturzyn by the Public School of his name, and a bass-relief in the local park, with the inscription: *Dedicated to the*

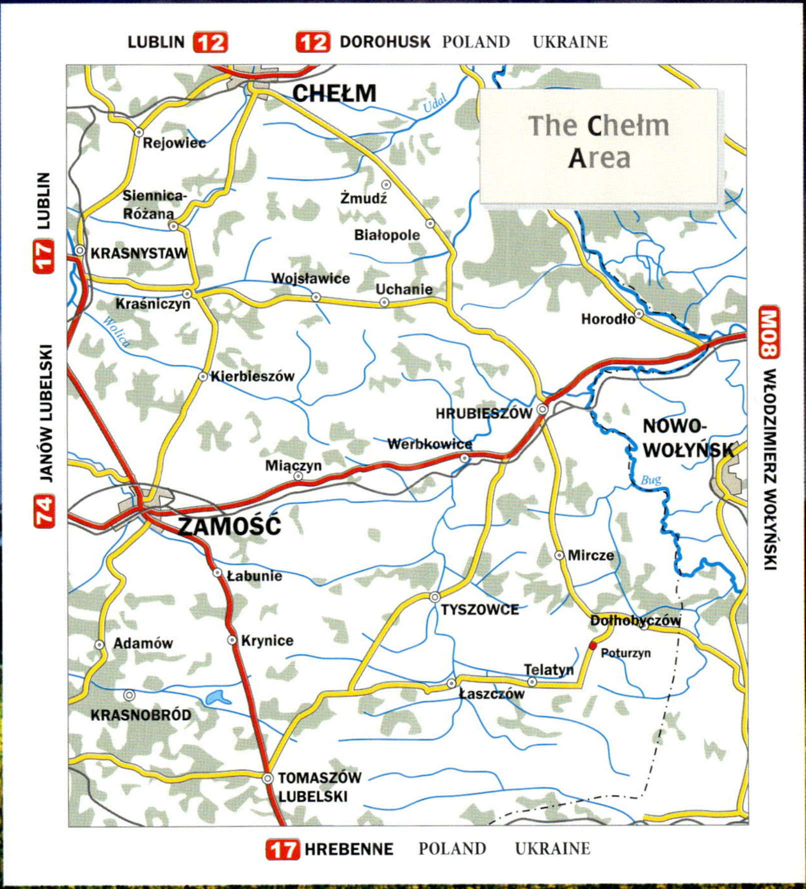

memory of Fryderyk Chopin, who stayed in Poturzyn at the house of his friend, Tytus Woyciechowski in the year 1830, soon before he left the country forever, carrying with him in his heart the folk songs of our people. PKZ Zamość, 1985.

The old manor house with the orangerie is no longer there; it was burned down during the war. The park grounds with the pond have grown wild and unkempt, the old trees have been cut down, and the only building remaining of the whole estate is the smithy. But, the Second World War destroyed more than just the buildings there. In 1944 the village became the site of a bloody suppression of the Polish people, who were murdered and buried in a mass grave by Ukrainian nationalists. Outside the village limits, where the woods once stood, is another mass grave – of soldiers who died in World War I – with a figure of Our Lady watching over them. There is one more small grave at its feet. It is dated 1860, and belongs to the daughter of Tytus Woyciechowski. According to one account of her death, she was murdered on that spot, and according to another she was bitten by a viper. Tytus Woyciechowski's remains rest in a family tomb at the cemetery in Oszczów, 10 km from Poturzyn.

Index of archival illustrations

p. 78
– **Jan Zamoyski**, ***Portrait of Ludwika Chopin***,1969; oil on canvas, 29 × 21.5 cm; reconstruction of the oil painting by Ambroży Mieroszewski from 1829; Frederic Chopin Museum collection at NIFC, property of TiFC

– **Jan Zamoyski**, ***Portrait of Izabella Chopin***, 1969; oil on canvas, 37 × 28.5 cm; reconstruction of the oil painting by Ambroży Mieroszewski from 1829; Frederic Chopin Museum collection at NIFC, property of TiFC

– **Artist unknown**, ***Portrait of Emilia Chopin***, ca. 1826-1827; miniature on ivory, watercolour and gouache, 7.2 × 4.2 cm; Frederic Chopin Museum collection at NIFC, property of TiFC

– **Napoleon Orda**, ***Żelazowa Wola***, litography from: *Album widoków historycznych Polski (An album of Poland's historic sites)*; Jagiellonian Library collection

p. 94 – **Fryderyk Chopin**, ***Kuryer Szafarski***; letters to family modelled after "Kurier Warszawski", 1824; autograph; Frederic Chopin Museum collection at NIFC, property of TiFC

pp. 100-101 – **Michał Stachowicz**, ***Harvest Festival***, 1821; 70 × 94 cm, oil on canvas; National Museum in Warsaw

p. 136 – **Eliza Radziwiłłówna**, ***Father's Room in Antonin***, pencil drawing, 18.9 × 25.8 cm; National Museum in Warsaw; repr. from *Chopin w kraju. Dokumenty i pamiątki*, collected and edited by K. Kobylańska, PWM, Kraków 1956

p. 138-139 – ***Chopin at the Radziwiłłs'***; rotogravure according to the painting by Henryk Siemiradzki; Jagiellonian University Museum

p. 143 – **Eliza Radziwiłłówna**, ***Portrait of Frederic Chopin***; pencil drawing on page 32 in album, 23.2 × 18.7 cm; Frederic Chopin Museum collection at NIFC

p. 146
– **Cracow. St. Florian's Gate**, ca. 1860; lithograph from life drawing by Henryk Walter; Jagiellonian Library collection

– **Fryderyk Dietrich**, ***Cracow. The Market Square***, 1817; aquatint; Jagiellonian Library collection

p. 152 – ***Pieskowa Rock***, steel engraving; Jagiellonian Library collection

pp. 154-155 – **Michał Stachowicz**, ***Tavern in Cracow***, 1819; oil on canvas, 33 × 92 cm; National Museum in Warsaw

Key:
NIFC – National Frederic Chopin Institute
PWM – Polskie Wydawnictwo Muzyczne /Polish Musical Publishing House
TiFC – Towarzystwo im. Fryderyka Chopina /Frederic Chopin Society

Selected bibliography

Andrzej Bukowski, *Pomorskie wojaże Chopina*, Marpress, Gdańsk 1993

Andrzej Bukowski, *Waplewo. Zapomniana placówka kultury polskiej na Pomorzu Nadwiślańskim*, Zakład Narodowy im. Ossolińskich, Wrocław 1989

Józef M. Chomiński, *Chopin*, PWM, Kraków 1978

Adam Czartkowski, Zofia Jeżewska, *Fryderyk Chopin*, PIW, Warszawa 1981

Maria Gordon Smith, George R. Marek, *Chopin*, Czytelnik, Warszawa, 1990

Ferdynand Hoesick, *Chopin. His Life and Work*, vol I – *Warszawa 1810–1831*, PWM 1967

Jarosław Iwaszkiewicz, *Chopin*, PIW, Warszawa 1949.

Zofia Jeżewska, *Chopin w kraju rodzinnym*, Wydawnictwo PTTK "Kraj", Warszawa 1985

Wacław Kmicic-Mieleszyński, *Sprawa pobytu Chopina w Gdańsku*, in: *The Book of the First International Congress Devoted to the Works of Frederick Chopin*, ed. Zofia Lissa, Warszawa 1963

Krystyna Kobylańska, *Korespondencja Fryderyka Chopina z rodziną*, PIW, Warszawa 1972

Artur Oppman, *Legendy warszawskie*, Wydawnictwo Zielona Sowa, Kraków 2008

Bronisław Edward Sydow, *Korespondencja Fryderyka Chopina*, vol 1-2, PIW, Warszawa 1955

Mieczysław Tomaszewski, *Chopin. Człowiek, dzieło, rezonans*, PWM, Kraków 2005

Bożena Weber, *Chopin*, Wydawnictwo Dolnośląskie, Wrocław 2000

Kazimierz Wierzyński, *Życie Chopina*, Wydawnictwo Literackie, Kraków 1978

Adam Zamoyski, *Chopin*, PIW, Warszawa, 1990

www.nifc.pl – Official Website of the National Fryderyk Chopin Institute

Following Chopin

Text
Kazimierz Kunicki
(pp. 7-11, 93-113, 131-143)
Tomasz Ławecki
(pp. 15-73, 123-127)
Liliana Olchowik-Adamowska
(pp. 76-91, 115-121, 145-161)

Photographs
Waldemar Panów
Zbigniew Panów
www.pzstudio.pl

Photographs on pp. 158-159
Adam Bujak

Graphic design
Tadeusz Nuckowski

Maps
Barbara Bączek
Władysław Bączek
"Meridian"

Editor
Joanna Kułakowska-Lis

English Translation
Agnieszka Topornicka

Proofreader
Thomas Crestodina

Printed by
Colonel, Kraków

Publisher
Wydawnictwo BOSZ

ISBN 978-83-7576-085-9

First Edition
Olszanica 2010

Wydawnictwo BOSZ
Office: ul. Przemysłowa 14
38-600 Lesko
tel. +48 13 4699000
fax +48 13 4696188
biuro@bosz.com.pl
www.bosz.com.pl